Indigenous Statistics

Indigenous Statistics

A Quantitative Research Methodology

Maggie Walter and Chris Andersen

Left Coast
Press Inc.

Walnut Creek, CA

Left Coast Press, Inc.
1630 North Main Street, #400
Walnut Creek, CA 94596
www.LCoastPress.com

ISBN 978-1-61132-292-7 hardcover
ISBN 978-1-61132-293-4 paperback
ISBN 978-1-61132-294-1 institutional eBook
ISBN 978-1-61132-697-0 consumer eBook

Library of Congress Cataloging-in-Publication Data

Walter, Maggie.
  Indigenous statistics : a quantitative research methodology / Maggie Walter, Chris Andersen.
    pages cm
  Summary: "In the first book ever published on Indigenous quantitative methodologies, Maggie Walter and Chris Andersen open up a major new approach to research across the disciplines and applied fields. While qualitative methods have been rigorously critiqued and reformulated, the population statistics relied on by virtually all research on Indigenous peoples continue to be taken for granted as straightforward, transparent numbers. This book dismantles that persistent positivism with a forceful critique, then fills the void with a new paradigm for Indigenous quantitative methods, using concrete examples of research projects from First World Indigenous peoples in the United States, Australia, and Canada. Concise and accessible, it is an ideal supplementary text as well as a core component of the methodological toolkit for anyone conducting Indigenous research or using Indigenous population statistics"—Provided by publisher.
  Includes bibliographical references and index.
  ISBN 978-1-61132-292-7 (hardback)—ISBN 978-1-61132-293-4 (paperback)—ISBN 978-1-61132-294-1 (institutional ebook)— ISBN 978-1-61132-697-0 consumer eBook
  1. Indigenous peoples—Statistics. 2. Indigenous peoples—Research—Methodology. I. Title.
  GN380.W35 2013
  305.80072'1–dc23
                    2013019759

Printed in the United States of America

♾™ The paper used in this publication meets the minimum requirements of American National Standard for Information Sciences—Permanence of Paper for Printed Library Materials, ANSI/NISO Z39.48–1992.

Cover design by Piper Wallis

Contents

Introduction

Statistics are powerful persuaders. As systematically collected numerical facts, they do much more than summarize reality in numbers. They also interpret reality and influence the way we understand society. The researchers who create statistics leave their mark on them—not just because people are biased in overt or conscious ways, but also because social, cultural, economic, and political perspectives infuse the research data even when we think we are "just counting people."

Population statistics in particular are an evidentiary base that reflects *and* constructs particular visions considered important in and to the modern state. They map the very contours of the social world itself. They shape and thus create the accepted reality of things most of us think they merely describe. Population statistics also play a powerful part in defining a nation's concept of itself. They map national social and economic trends empirically: education levels; age and gender distributions; patterns of birth, morbidity and mortality; labor market figures; income dynamics; and many other phenomena. Via this mapping process they provide to the nation-state and its various populations a portrait of themselves. The social, cultural, and economic phenomena that are chosen for inclusion, and also those which are excluded, provide a reflection of the nation-state's changing social, cultural, and economic priorities and norms.

For example, up until the 1980s it was the norm in census questions relating to household structure in Western nations such as Australia, the United Kingdom, and the United States of America to categorize the male adult as the household head and the female adult as a dependent. Changes in the Western social norms around gender during the 1960s and 1970s led to changes in

Indigenous Statistics: A Quantitative Research Methodology by Maggie Walter and Chris Andersen, 7–20. © 2013 Left Coast Press, Inc. All rights reserved.

how household data were sought within the census. From the 1986 census, in Australia, for instance, any adult, male or female, in a household could be nominated as Person 1 on the census form (ASSDA n.d.). Likewise, in Canada changing definitions of the kinds of ethnicities that people could locate themselves in on the census played a role in the kinds of arguments they could make to government because they lacked "scientific" data to back up their claims.

For Indigenous peoples, especially in first world countries where population statistics powerfully influence governance and social services, these numbers have become a foundational lens through which we, as Indigenous people and peoples, become known to our respective nation-states and how we engage in many of our relationships with government actors. Statistics are used to describe our population profiles and geographical distribution, and, almost universally across the colonized first world, our lagging levels of educational achievement, labor market participation, health, and economic status. They are nation-states' chief tool for ascertaining and presenting the official "who," "what," "where," and "how" of Indigenous life. Often positioned as a subset of overall national social trends, these data are accepted as a straightforward, objective snapshot of an underlying reality. As such, they have also become the backbone for the creation and implementation of social policy for Indigenous peoples.

Australian census data on homelessness, for example, with their pattern of heavy over-representation of Indigenous peoples recorded among the homeless, influence government homelessness policy shape and program function (ISSR 2012). In Canada, census data are used to produce the formulas with which the Canadian government and various Aboriginal organizations calculate funding for Canada's Aboriginal employment and training programs and, increasingly, for post-secondary education for certain classifications of Aboriginal students (HRSDC 2004). In the United States, Census Bureau reports on where and how Native Americans live are a key factor in policy decisions on how best to deliver social services (Fonseca 2012).

In a very real sense, statistics also increasingly frame Indigenous understandings. As we invest ourselves and our communities in their categories, we increasingly use statistics to help us tell *ourselves* who we are. For example, the data collected by the United States Census Bureau that enumerate Native American and Alaska Native populations are used by tribal groups to plan the infrastructure needed to meet tribal government responsibilities (Census Bureau 2012). Equally importantly, however, members of these populations recognize ourselves *empirically* in these depictions. In Australia, for example, population data appear to confirm not only that Aboriginal and Torres Strait Islander peoples are growing as a proportion of the overall population, but also that we are increasingly urban (AIHW 2011a). Likewise, in Canada statistics have been used by Indigenous political leaders to document the long-standing gaps in our respective qualities of life. Statistics, therefore, do not

just describe reality—they create it. In doing so, they not only influence how the phenomena they describe are understood, they also shape their accepted explanations.

Three Premises

This book is based on three central premises that we will preface here. These premises that speak to issues regarding the cultural framework of Indigenous statistics, the methodologies that produce them, and understanding academia as a situated activity. Though we discuss them throughout the book, we would nonetheless like to preface them here.

The Cultural Framework of Indigenous Statistics

The first premise is that the quantitative methodologies that guide the collection, analysis, and interpretation of data about Indigenous peoples both reflect and constitute, in ways largely invisible to their producers and users, the dominant cultural framework of the nation-state within which they (that is, statistics) operate. Although the statistical depictions used to summarize the social complexity of Indigenous communities (all communities, for that matter) are neither natural nor normal, the cultural weight and power of statistical techniques and the numerical summaries they generate speak a "truth" about the communities on which they shine their statistical light. But the way that they shine that light pushes out other ways of conceiving about and acting upon those communities. In a straightforward Foucauldian sense, statistics—and official statistics in particular—operate as a powerful truth claim in most modern societies.

How does this apply to Indigenous peoples in particular? At the risk of belaboring this point, we argue that rather than representing neutral numerics, quantitative data play a powerful role in *constituting* reality through their underpinning methodologies by virtue of the social, cultural, and racial terrain in which they are conceived, collected, analysed, and interpreted. For Indigenous peoples in first world nations in particular (for reasons we discuss later), population statistics operate as a primary vehicle for majority non-Indigenous understandings of the minority Indigene in their midst (and for that matter, within Indigenous communities as well). As Māori scholar Tahu Kukutai (2011: 47) states, within the world of data, Indigenous populations are "statistical creations based on aggregated individual-level data, rather than 'real world' concrete groups."

Nonetheless, Indigenous statistics still define our relationship with our respective nation-states as though they constituted real things. The epistemological gap erased in failing to differentiate between social relations and the statistics that draw estimates about them has effectively constituted the public Indigene in ways that, more often than not, are comparatively pejorative, tending toward a documentation of difference, deficit, and dysfunction. Of course, very real and enduring problems *do* get reflected in statistics, but the major failing of current statistical methodologies is that they tend to *only* understand us according to these terms. Not only are Indigenous peoples constituted as "the problem," non-Indigenous ways of life are left uncritiqued, despite the fact that in many cases current consumer lifestyles are environmentally unsustainable (to provide one example of many).

Methodologies Produce Indigenous Statistics

The book's second premise is that we need to differentiate between *methods* and *methodologies*. We argue that it is the methodologies within which data are collected, analysed, and interpreted that shape the picture that the statistics produce, rather than the research method of statistical analysis itself. Methodology is the active element in constituting the portrait of the realities that statistical techniques eventually create; it determines why and how particular research questions are asked (and why others are not); how, when, and where the data are gathered; how they are explored; and how the resulting data are interpreted and, significantly, eventually used. With statistics at the base of most comparative analyses of social relations, for researchers in any discipline, qualitative or quantitative, understanding how statistics are created and deployed—in everything from social service delivery and governance to cultural affairs and personal identity—is crucial to being able to understand them as social constructions and, therefore, to being able to fashion alternatives.

Academic Research Is a Situated Activity

The book's third and final premise—written in the spirit of emphasizing what Indigenous qualitative and quantitative methods share in common—is that we need to be more cognizant of the translative processes through which non-academic knowledge is translated into the academy. In other words, while many qualitative researchers (Indigenous or otherwise) position their work as anathema to statistical research, we both remain invested in the sets of power relations specific to the academy. Therefore, when Indigenous qualitative researchers speak to the importance of cultural markers without accounting for the particular forms of translation or refraction that occur—*must* occur—for their use in academic scholarship, they elide important conversations about the differences between "community" and "academic" knowledge. Equally, quantitative resources who fail to attend to these differences make the same mistake.

By emphasizing the underlying similarity of qualitative and quantitative academic knowledge, we are not suggesting that real differences do not exist. It is thus probably useful to lay out what we see as the key differences. For us, *qualitative* methodologies tend to focus on small or localized objectives and to examine them more deeply, analysing subjective experiences with a level of contextualization and depth, often over a long period of time. The point of qualitative methodologies is to situate the objects of analysis (a term not often used in qualitative research) in terms of the subjective feelings of their participants. In sociology, for example, qualitative methods are associated with the ground-breaking work of feminist scholars who attempted to demonstrate how contemporaneous male-dominated statistical research tended to cut out women's voices from the statistical "truths" they created. Likewise, many of the categories used to collect the data reflected male understandings (see Firestone 1972; Ortner 1974; Pateman 1991).

Quantitative research, in contrast, tends toward the numerical. Probably the most important element of this methodology is that it *abstracts*. That is, these methodologies allow researchers to draw information from local context, standardize it, and, removing it from context, deliver it to a central point of calculation (Curtis 2001: 31). Quantitative methodologies facilitate standardization and render information specific to local social relations both mobile and combinable. In this way, what is seen as the "messiness" of local context can be removed, ordered, scaled, compared, and rearranged as required by researchers (2001: 31). This reordering and rescaling is used to draw conclusions about larger numbers of people and broader sets of social relations (like "the city," "the nation," "the Western world," or, in this case, "the Indigenous population"). It is the issue of abstraction that appears to cause the most consternation among qualitative researchers, who suggest that this philosophical orientation tends to miss the complexity of our social relations in pursuit of broad macro-level patterns, tendencies, and summaries. It also seems to downplay the importance of "place," central to many expressions of Indigeneity.

As one of this book's reviewers rightly pointed out, quantitative methodologies are far broader than the specific subset we use in this book: official statistics. From a methodological point of view, censuses are distinctive among quantitative data in that they do not require methodological discussions (or methods) about *sampling*. Likewise, they need not worry in the same way about issues of *representation*—that is, the idea that a sample is generalizable to a broader population. By definition, populations are not representative[1]—they constitute the broader "group" that a representative sample would wish to speak on behalf of. In this book we focus specifically on issues of population and large scale survey data because, although quantitative samples carry their own forms of legitimacy, census estimates and national surveys carry far and away the greatest weight when it comes to talking about empirical depictions of Indigenous qualities-of-life and the forms of social policy that engage with their findings.

Indigeneity and the Statistical Lens

We can immediately understand why Indigenous peoples in general, Indigenous scholars in particular, and those using qualitative methodologies would view quantitative methodologies with suspicion. Especially in the context of official data like those found in the census and other government databases, historical data collectors often had only the barest relationships with those whose information they collected. Moreover, government taxonomies tended to reflect the times they were constructed in such that official classifications had little to do with the highly contextual collective self-understandings of Indigenous peoples themselves. For example, in his discussion of historical state construction in South Asia, Benedict Anderson argued that "it is extremely unlikely that… more than a tiny fraction of those categorized and subcategorized would have recognized themselves under [state] labels. These 'identities', imagined by the (confusedly) classifying mind of the colonial state, still awaited the reification which imperial administrative penetration would soon make possible" (Anderson 1991: 165).

Anderson's (1991) point that official classifications reflect(ed) administrative desires rather than on-the-ground realities—despite their power to render such categories "real"—has obvious links to Foucault's concept of *discourse* as practices (seemingly in a way slightly different than pointed out earlier) that do not describe objects but rather "constitute them and in doing so conceal their own invention" (1972: 49). We note, too, a broad "governmentality" literature that explores the links between governance, identity, and statistics (see Barry et al. 1996; Burshell et al. 2001; Curtis 2001; Dean 2010; Rose 1999: ch. 6). In particular, Foucault and others have argued that statistics represented a central technology through which social relations were rendered "governable." Foucault (1991) fundamentally predicated the birth and legitimacy of modern, liberal forms of power on the calculated production of standardized knowledge useful for administrative intervention into a new object of governance: "the population."

In this context, statistics have come to play a central role. Coterminous with the growth of "bio-power," Foucault (1991) differentiated between what he termed an "art of government" geared towards intervening upon and regulating the citizenry as a whole ("the population") and the "micro-power" of discipline which acts upon individual bodies. Statistics were thought central to the practice of liberalism, which we broadly conceive as including a concern with limiting the exercise of formal state power while developing the capacities of liberty among that power's citizens. In this sense, "population" was thought to represent naturally occurring phenomena that possessed their own autonomy and internally produced regularities (Burshell 1991: 126; Foucault 1991).

Importantly, in avoiding the risks inherent in over-governing, population-based statistics allowed liberal government authorities to respect the natural autonomy of certain "private zones," like market economies and civil society (Rose 1999: 49), while concomitantly shaping the activities within those zones according to certain objectives: "good government depended on the well-being of these domains; hence political authorities simultaneously acquired the obligation to foster self-organizing capacities of those natural spheres" (Rose 1999: 49). Liberal government was ultimately about how to best make efficient use of the natural capacities of populations and their members without over-interfering (see Foucault 1991). Hindess (2001, 2004, 2008) notes, however, that while early liberal thought focused on how best to govern in ways that guaranteed the liberty of those being governed, these rationalities presupposed a certain capacity to benefit from and contribute to that liberty. Using Adam Smith's discussion of market economies as an example, Hindess explains how collective interactions in the market were seen to foster, in an internal and self-regulated manner, values of prudence, autonomy, and self-direction. While these figured centrally in the reproduction of a "civilized" society, they necessarily presupposed individuals endowed with the *capacity* for such prudence, autonomy, and self-direction. In other words, only certain subjects were endowed with the capacity to benefit from the kind of liberalism that population-based governance helped bring about and then shepherd.

Hindess (2004) offers a second key insight: liberalism's authoritarian elements (what he terms its "unfreedom") cannot be understood as contradictory or aberrational to an otherwise enlightened form of rule. Rather, they speak centrally to its *developmentally based* notion of human capacity: government works best by making use of these capacities, and, as such, liberal authority required the discretion "to distinguish between what can be governed through the promotion of liberty and what must be governed in other ways" (Hindess 2004: 28). Perhaps unsurprisingly, early liberal theorists positioned Western civilization, with its form of civil society and exchange-based market economy, as most likely to foster the natural capacities of liberal subjects. As such, it was thought to represent the apex of civilized society.

Presupposing the capacity of subjects to bear (certain forms of) liberty enabled liberal authorities to confidently distinguish between populations suitable for liberal rule and those requiring more authoritarian forms of governance. Certain "non-liberal" populations were thought unable to produce the capacity required to be ruled according to liberal ideals. Both preferable and necessary to liberal rule in certain cases, authoritarian rule was thought to ensure the steady advancement of colonial locales and populations towards the European/metropolitan norms of civilization: "Despotism…is a legitimate mode of government in dealing with barbarians, provided the end be their improvement" (J. S. Mill, in Li 2007: 14). Far from representing an irony or a contradiction of liberalism, then, authoritarianism constituted a necessary colonial potentiality, and Indigenous nations and communities were often the main targets of these forms of authoritative intervention.

Colonial authoritarianism represented a key plank in the global practice of liberalism, but that doesn't tell us much about what it looked like in practice. In his discussion of "colonial governmentality," Scott (1995: 196) critiques the imprecision of Partha Chatterjee's (1993) famous characterization of colonial power as rooted in a "rule of difference." Chatterjee argued that classifying differences marked a dividing line in the colonial dialectic of dominance and subservience, civilized and savage, self and other (also see McClintock 1995; Said 1978, 1993). While sympathetic to Chatterjee's analysis, Scott argued that even if the *fact* of this rule of exclusion generally holds true across time and space, it tells us nothing about the *form* it takes. Scott asked instead: "What are the specific power-effects of race? How was it inserted into subject-constituting practices, into the formation of certain kinds of "raced" subjectivities?" (1995: 196). In this sense, important—and more precise—questions emerge regarding who was targeted, how they were targeted, what effects or outcomes were prescribed, and what practicalities eventually emerged. Statistics played a central role in making these historical determinations, just as they continue to resonate in powerful ways today.

Despite its theoretical density, governmentality literature is thus useful for thinking about statistics as something other than neutrally describing artifacts. They hold real power to help constitute a social world that most of us more or less take for granted, and this is probably particularly the case in the context of communities that do not hold the power to produce their own statistical counter-realities, as is the case in most Indigenous communities. As the weight of statistical representations and the massive amount of policy reports and academic scholarship which make use of them begin to pile up, the sheer volume of the work tends to stand in for the more complex realities that sit beneath it. In an Indigenous context, in the hands of state actors and scholars with little practical knowledge about the peoples their statistics analyze, these reports have produced very narrow but largely accepted lenses through which most people think about and "understand" Indigenous peoples today.

Using the idea of a lens to think about statistical issues may seem slightly strange. In fact, it is surprisingly apt. Many of us who have gone to see an optometrist or an ophthalmologist for an eye examination have heard the refrain "better, or worse?" as he or she attempted to calculate our sight deficiencies. This process helps them determine the correct eyeglass prescription. Unlike eyeglasses, there is no external standard to which populations can be submitted to determine if they are "true, or not true." Nonetheless, in a very real way censuses operate as a kind of lens through which we look at the social world. Different questions, different enumerators, different enumeratees—each shapes, in a metaphorical way, the kind of lens through which we look at the world. Thus, like eyeglass lenses, censuses do not simply reflect the social world: they refract it.

In addition to understanding the power of statistics for shaping the social world and its role in how governing takes place in nation-states, this book is also rooted in a second set of theoretical precepts. Indebted to the work of Foucault's contemporary Pierre Bourdieu, the discourse we refer to throughout the following chapters emerges from the dominant *habitus* of producers and users of statistical data peculiar to first world colonized nations, such as the United States, Canada, Australia, or Aotearoa New Zealand. Habitus, as Bourdieu (1984) explains, is the coalescence of our social dispositions: the set of beliefs, attitudes, skills, and practices possessed and employed by individuals in their daily life. Our dispositions are shaped by our position in three dimensional social space, a position delineated by our social, cultural, and economic capital positioning. As argued elsewhere (see Walter 2010c), we add race as a fourth dimension of social space, and in settler states in particular, perceive Indigeneity or settler majority origins as a central aspect of a society's race capital continuum. Our habitus not only shapes our worldview but also our life chances, and while we act as individuals, our life trajectories and our dispositions are likely similar to others with a similar habitus.

Most critical for our purpose is Bourdieu's (1984) argument that an individual's habitus is not a set of attributes and attitudes that is consciously worked out. Rather, it directs action largely unconsciously through beliefs that, while internalized, are nonetheless derived from external social forces. Thus, the social practices engendered by a particular habitus appear to the individuals involved in those social practices to be natural and normal, as "just the way things are." In Bourdieu's words, they possess a "synthetic unity" (1984: 173). Our central argument, therefore, is that the colonial habitus of the settler majority (who are the primary producers and users of Indigenous statistics) shapes the dominant quantitative methodological practices in these countries and that this habitus constitutes Indigenous statistics in a particular way. Equally importantly, we claim that as Indigenous policy actors and others become increasingly *invested* in statistical categories, the categories become naturalized by nearly all who make use of them. As Bourdieu might phrase it, they lose the forest for the trees.

It is in this way that dominant methodologies emerge from the dominant cultural framework of the society of their instigators and users. The quantitative methodologies predominantly used within nation-states that have colonized Indigenous peoples, therefore, are those of the colonizer. This is not meant as a depreciatory statement but, rather, as a simple fact. All quantitative methodologies are historical, cultural, and racial artifacts—they cannot be otherwise. A key concern of this book, therefore, is to demonstrate that it is not possible to differentiate an Indigenous quantitative methodology without first delineating the predominant methodology with which the Indigenous quantitative methodologies will be compared and contrasted.

Current mainstream statistical methodologies also largely fail to provide a vehicle for Indigenous peoples to understand, portray, and constitute ourselves statistically. This is not to argue that current statistical data that focus on Indigenous issues are inaccurate or worthless. Statistical techniques are not only important research methods, they are methods that require considerable expertise and long hours of analysis to achieve rigorous results. Rather, our argument is that many of these data, as they currently exist, tend to constitute Indigenous peoples as *deficient* and that these portrayals can, and do, restrict and inhibit other ways of understanding or using statistical data by, and for, Indigenous peoples. The other concern of this book, therefore, is to define, conceptualize, and operationalize Indigenous quantitative methodologies in ways that stimulate the imagining of quantitative research that operates within, and reflects, Indigenous historical, cultural, and racial methodological values, priorities, and frameworks. Our aim is to support the construction of alternative Indigenous statistical portraits and narratives, ones that accord with Indigenous worldviews and interests. Moreover, and perhaps more controversially, we will demonstrate that quantitative methodologies reflect aspects of our contemporary selves every bit as Indigenous as those of qualitative methodologies.

In these contexts, the book proceeds according to two questions:

1. How can quantitative research methods be integrated into an Indigenous methodological frame?
2. What would such quantitative research look like in practice—how would it differ from "business as usual"?

The Structure of Our Book

It should be clear to readers that the straightforward adoption of standard quantitative methodological practice by Indigenous researchers is not in itself enough to constitute an Indigenous quantitative framework. An Indigenous researcher undertaking quantitative research does not by any measure translate into Indigenous quantitative methodological practice. Rather, as we argue in more detail in the coming chapters, Indigenous quantitative research is in essence quantitative research framed and developed from an Indigenous socially positioned, epistemological, ontological, and axiological perspective (see Moreton-Robinson and Walter 2010). This is not as simple as: "add Indigeneity and stir." Rather, approaching quantitative research from an Indigenous frame is a methodologically transformative process that acknowledges *all* of our (Indigenous and non-) central presence in contemporary global modernity and does not assume that a movement *toward* modernity necessarily means a move *away* from Indigeneity.

This book articulates this process and this presence. To our knowledge this is the only book that takes Indigenous quantitative methodologies as its subject. It is also one of the few writings in the broader field of Indigenous methodologies to move beyond what Indigenous methodologies are to how they are actually practiced. Our purpose is to provide a directly applicable resource for researchers, one that includes, but reaches beyond, theorizing philosophy and underpinning methodological and paradigmatic principles to conceptually and pragmatically map Indigenous research quantitative methodology practices and processes.

We start in the next chapter by demonstrating how dominant quantitative methodologies fail Indigenous peoples and their nation-states. Narrow and pejorative delineations of Indigenous peoples play a key role in perpetuating the colonizing framework in first world nations. In Chapter 2 we do what most research books do not: we define and conceptualize methodology as a critical prerequisite of our articulation of an Indigenous quantitative methodological frame. In Chapter 3 we begin the process of conceptualizing an Indigenous quantitative methodology by exploring and setting the parameters of this paradigm. Here we argue for an accounting of modernity within first world Indigenous methodologies; we also argue against positioning Indigenous methodology dichotomously in opposition to Western frames and against grounding it in a concept of traditional knowledge and culture "outside of modernity."

Following this, Chapters 4 and 5 operationalize Indigenous quantitative methodology using case studies drawn from actual research conducted by the authors. Chapter 4 demonstrates *nayri kati*, an Australian-based Indigenous quantitative methodology, and in Chapter 5 Indigenous quantitative methodological practice is operationalized in a Canadian context. In the final chapter we argue the urgent case for a greater take up of quantitative research by Indigenous researchers and scholars and our allies around the globe.

Indigenous Peoples in this Book

Given the diversity of Indigenous peoples, the United Nations Permanent Forum on Indigenous Issues (UNPFII) declines to adopt an official definition of Indigenous. Instead, the body proposes a "modern understanding of this term based on the following: self-identification as indigenous peoples at the individual level and accepted by the community as their member; historical continuity with pre-colonial and/or pre-settler societies; strong link to territories and surrounding natural resources; distinct social, economic or political systems; distinct language, culture and beliefs; form non-dominant groups of society; resolve to maintain and reproduce their ancestral environments and systems as distinctive peoples and communities" (UNPFII n.d.).

This non-definition has led to the frequent use, by those wishing to define Indigenous peoples (see Axelsson and Skold 2011 for example), of the 1987 working definition formulated by Jose R. Martinez Cobo (at the time a UN special rapporteur):

> Indigenous communities, peoples and nations are those which, having a historical continuity with pre-invasion and pre-colonial societies that developed on their territories, consider themselves distinct from other sectors of the societies now prevailing on those territories, or parts of them. They form at present non-dominant sectors of society and are determined to preserve, develop and transmit to future generations their ancestral territories, and their ethnic identity, as the basis of their continued existence as peoples, in accordance with their own cultural patterns, social institutions and legal system. (1987: Add 4, paras 379 and 381)

We accept the central premises of the UNPFII's criteria and Martinez Cobo's definition, but this book is written primarily in reference to the subgroup of Indigenous peoples whose own nations have been subsumed through colonization into Western first world nation-states because we believe that the liberalism which shapes these governing rhetorics requires a particular relationship with population statistics not (as) present in other global contexts (see Rose 1999: ch. 6). These Indigenous peoples fit also within with Dyck's (1985) definition of fourth world peoples as those who:

- are Indigenous to the lands that form the nation state;
- have had their sovereignty and territory appropriated by settler colonialism;
- are economically and politically marginalized;
- have their Indigenous culture stigmatized by the dominant culture;
- are struggling for social justice and for a right to self-determination and control over their traditional lands and resources; and
- constitute a tiny minority of the population of a nation, contributing to their political powerlessness.

Australian Aboriginal and Torres Strait Islanders, American Indians, Canadian Aboriginals, Māori, Inuit and Sami, Native Hawaiians, some peoples from Pacific Islands and some Arctic peoples—among others—fit these criteria.

In this text, however, we use the term "colonized first world Indigenous peoples" because of the centrality of the shared colonized histories and contemporary social, economic, and political positioning of Indigenous peoples living in Western colonized first world nations and how the dominant quantitative methodologies currently position these peoples. Of course, we believe that our analysis and methodologies are useful to other Indigenous peoples. But because methodologies cannot be conceptualized or operationalized in isolation from an understanding of their historical, cultural, and racial antecedents, we are careful not to assume that our analysis applies wholesale to the vast diversity of Indigenous peoples outside of our own personal and research experience. "Indigenous" is an umbrella term; it encompasses many different peoples living in many different nation-states, and many different social, political, and cultural circumstances. Thus, our term, colonized first world Indigenous peoples, is a useful heuristic that recognizes certain shared characteristics, but we still recognize diversity of peoples within this category, as well as connections and continuities with peoples outside this category.

Likewise, we emphasize, with many qualitative Indigenous methodology scholars, the importance of "place" to situating Indigeneity (see Battiste and Henderson 2000; Deloria and Wildcat 2001; Evans et al. forthcoming; Hart 2010; Kovach 2009). The otherwise legitimate emphasis on place has, however, marginalized what we see as two important contextual elements. First, "place" is itself always contextual and always a matter of scale—for example, we might take a local Indigenous settlement as an example of place that holds deep ceremonial meaning to those who live or are from there. However, Indigenous places are also, in many cases, "large." Whether we're talking about urban Aboriginal communities—remember, almost *all* cities were Indigenous spaces first—or about larger rural locales, statistical methods are in many cases more suitable to the research issues we seek answers to.

Second, Indigenous peoples are *modern* and we are heavily invested in that modernity. We will have more to say about this issue in later chapters, but here we want to flag the fact that many of the abstractions that some might think sit in opposition to Indigenous methodologies—often exemplified in government administrative categories of Indigeneity, for example—are already abstractions that we recognize our selves in, both singularly and collectively. This investment is a necessary evil of living in modern nation-states, what Métis scholar Paul Chartrand (1991) has termed our "captor nations." Therefore, to suggest that the kinds of abstractions that statisticians (must) engage in are innately anti-Indigenous is to ignore the extent to which we have already legitimized them in our daily lives.

We have written this book using primarily Australian and Canadian examples because it is in these places that our scholarship and Indigeneity are grounded. From time to time we make use of examples from Hawaii, the rest of the United States, and Aotearoa New Zealand, but we remain mindful that we do not have scholarly expertise nor the Indigenous understandings to legitimately center these places in our arguments. Nonetheless, presenting Canadian and Australian Indigenous realities provides a powerful proxy for other colonized first world nations. Indigenous Australia and Canada are geographically on different continents; and the heritage, culture, and traditions of our various peoples have no common Indigenous antecedents. As detailed above, however, what we share is the governing rationalities of our colonizers, and it is this that shapes our contemporaneous similarity. Our argument is, thus, that if Indigenous peoples as diverse as those from Canada and Australia share Indigenous quantitative methodological commonalities, then it is highly likely that other Colonized First World Indigenous peoples will also in ways that, if not identical, are analogous.

Conclusion: Take the Indigenous Quantitative Journey

As a final introductory word we want to emphasize that our book is not intended to be for the exclusive use of Indigenous researchers. Indigenous quantitative methodologies are open to all who wish to undertake research. Indeed, understanding and observing how we rearticulate, reframe, redefine, redesign, and re-practice quantitative methodologies within Indigenous worldviews may prove revelatory for *all* quantitative practitioners, Indigenous and non-Indigenous alike. The journey is not, however, without its challenges. In reading this book you are entering Indigenous statistical space, whether as a new researcher or as a long-standing ally. Some non-Indigenous researchers in particular may feel unsettled by entering such a "raced" space where you are the subject of, rather than the definer of, how racial categories are statistically explored. Unconsciousness of dominant cultural, social, and racial norms can make turning the analytical lens 180 degrees away from its examination of the 'other' to being examined as the 'other' threatening. But it is also liberating. We welcome and encourage you to take the journey with us.

Note

1 This issue is actually more complicated than this. As internal demography debates make clear, different standards exist for more or less trustworthy analyses of population data.

Chapter 1

Deficit Indigenes

Introduction

This chapter explores how dominant quantitative methodologies shortchange Indigenous communities. We use Canadian and Australian examples from our own work to explore how statistical constructions of Indigeneity are played out on a terrain of *racialization*[1] specific to Canada's and Australia's colonial contexts. We know from discussions with our colleagues in Aotearoa New Zealand, the continental United States, Hawaii, and those nation-states that now encompass Sami lands that the issues we identify in this chapter are directly pertinent to their own experiences and understandings of how Indigenous statistics are done. These issues are, we argue, part of the broader effects of colonialism on the investment of Indigenous identity in statistical forms, which are not specific to individual nation-states. Rather, we restrict the nation-state frame of our discussion because that is the limit of our expertise, and we do not wish to speak for other first world colonized Indigenous peoples.

Development literature dominates contemporary discussions about research on Indigenous communities across first world colonizing nation-states. What is less discussed, however, is the central role of statistics and statistical analysis within the development discourse and policy action. What we highlight in this chapter is how the categories utilized to collect data are methodologically configured to produce only certain kinds of data. In both Canada and Australia, the guiding quantitative methodology rather than the quantitative method itself shapes and limits the data and their utility. The outcome is that rather than presenting numerical pictures of reality, as they are usually portrayed, Indigenous statistics become intensely political. Methodologically, they are colonizer-settler artifacts that serve their masters and disserve their subjects, and they do so in a manner that has become the norm, and as such, requires little thought or consciousness about their restrictiveness.

The Neo-Colonial Alliance of Statistics and Policy

In Canada and Australia, statistics about Indigenous peoples are enmeshed in discourses associated with long-standing government policies that aim to "close the (socioeconomic) gap" between Aboriginal and non-Indigenous populations. The unacknowledged power relations inherent in these discourses position the Indigenous population as in need of being 'brought up' to the non-Indigenous standard in educational, labor market, and other socio-economic indicators, and produce statistical configurations anchored in development or deficit-based understandings of Indigenous peoples and communities. There is an extensive literature documenting the evolution of development studies, its explicit roots in modernity, and the colonial projects that comprise it as a field (see, for example, Desai and Potter 2002; Kothari 2005; Peet and Hartwick 2009). This literature documents the discursive shift between colonial and contemporary times of perceiving the 'problem' of Indigenous people from one of inconvenient continued existence and biological inferiority to one of inconvenient cultural uniqueness and culturally linked behavioral deviation.

In both Canada and Australia, the contemporary response to the statistically defined Indigenous problem is the creation and longstanding presence of a massive public policy infrastructure. This infrastructure is primarily dedicated to accurately measuring the "developmental lag" of "their" Indigenous communities and ruminating on how to best govern and "fix" our seemingly endemic problems and chronic conditions. This has been termed as "demography of disadvantage" (Jones 2004; Taylor 2004). In Canada, for example, the federal government likes to tout that it spends billions yearly on alleviating these conditions, allocations most recently geared toward health, employment, and training. In Australia, officials similarly recently pointed to an investment of more than nine billion dollars to be expended over the next six to ten years on behalf of Indigenous Australians (FAHCSIA 2012).

Historically, as liberal nation-states moved out of explicit administrative attempts to *assimilate* Indigenous communities toward a more integrative colonialism that assumed that Indigenous peoples would (want to) become an economic and political part of the nation-state, government policy began to dedicate itself to improving the social and material conditions of Indigenous communities and individuals. Gone was the era of targeted surveillance and disciplinary measures like those found in Church- or state-run schools for Indigenous children. Increasingly, Aboriginal communities were incorporated into an expanding policy ethos that presupposed that we could and should participate in modern life—but only if we were willing to do so within its increasingly narrow norms (see Shewell 2008).

Along these lines, welfare "improvement" programs were fashioned, and program officers intervened into Aboriginal communities in the context of these new rationalities. Of course, given classic liberalism's conflation of moral improvement with economic productivity, accompanying these changing rationalities were government-initiated "grand schemes of development that affected resources and Indigenous peoples in 'peripheral areas'. These included, among others, agrarian reform, agricultural colonization, green revolution schemes, road building, dams, mining and oil exploration and production" (Blazer et al. 2004: 6) in both countries and efforts to "normalize" many predominantly Aboriginal or Torres Strait Islander communities via the introduction of good governance, self reliance, and self support schemes (such as the Community Development Employment Scheme) in Australia (Petersen and Sanders 1998) and the so-called "White Paper" in Canada (Chretien 2011 [1969]).

If statistical information was increasingly crucial to the modern governing of Aboriginal communities in Canada and Australia, however, the categories through which such information was (and is) collected and analyzed remained firmly rooted in the administrative ideals of previous eras. While the changing rationalities of government shifted the kinds of relationships through which government officials attempted to engage with Indigenous communities, per capita investment in these communities—in the absence, incidentally, of any sustained input from the Indigenous communities into which it was to be invested—remained much lower than that invested into non-Indigenous communities in both countries (see Milloy 2008 for a Canadian discussion; see Altman et al. 2008 for an Australian one). Thus, these newly "integrative" governing rationalities took place almost entirely at the pace of government and, over time, helped produce the conditions of an increasingly low quality of life for many Indigenous individuals, families, and communities.

To rationalize and measure their process, since the 1960s for Canada and the 1970s for Australia, succeeding government administrations have commissioned numerous official reports documenting, and making suggestions for improving, the conditions of their respective Aboriginal populations. In Canada, this era began with the publication of the *Hawthorn Report* in 1966, and though continuing today, was again brought to the forefront of public attention with the 1996 publication of the *Royal Commission on Aboriginal Peoples*. This thirty-year era has apparently convincingly demonstrated the tremendous gap between Aboriginal and non-Aboriginal Canadians. For example, in the mid-1960s the authors of the *Hawthorn Report* originally wrote that "it has become increasingly evident in recent years...that the majority of the Indian population constitutes a group economically depressed in terms of the standards that have become widely accepted in Canada…[and] there are indications that the gap between the two groups is widening" (1966 part 1: 21). Thirty years later, the *Royal Commission on Aboriginal Peoples* (1996) stated that while conditions in our communities had improved since 1966, a massive gap still existed in relation to the quality of life of non-Aboriginal Canadians, characterized by social conditions in which:

> Life expectancy is lower. Illness is more common. Human problems, from family violence to alcohol abuse, are more common too. Fewer children graduate from high school. Far fewer go on to colleges and universities. The homes of Aboriginal people are more often flimsy, leaky and overcrowded. Water and sanitation systems in Aboriginal communities are more often inadequate. Fewer Aboriginal people have jobs. More spend time in jails and prisons.[2]

To give one example of this apparently dire picture, below is a graph (Figure 1.1) of the differential between the Aboriginal and the non-Aboriginal Community Well-Being Index (CWI). The CWI measures the relative quality of life of First Nations and Inuit communities in comparison to non-Aboriginal communities in Canada. Four indicators shape this measure: education, labor

Figure 1.1: The Community Well-Being Index (CWI): Measuring Well-Being in First Nations and Non-Aboriginal Communities, 1981–2006.

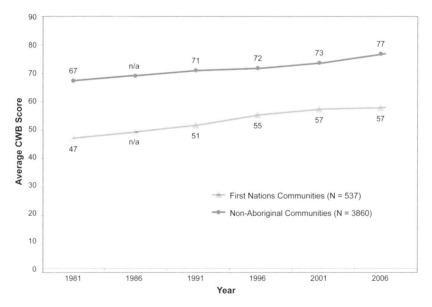

Source: Aboriginal Affairs and Northern Development Canada, 2011. Reproduced with the permission of the Minister of Aboriginal Affairs and Northern Development Canada, 2013.

force participation, income, and a qualitative and quantitative housing measure (see O'Sullivan 2011). Though for First Nations only, the CWI figure demonstrates convincingly that while the quality of life measures for First Nations and non-Aboriginal communities have both grown steadily over the past three decades, the quality of life for First Nations still remains far below that for non-Aboriginals.

Similarly, in Australia Indigenous statistics are a core business of the national government statistical agencies, the Australian Bureau of Statistics (ABS), and the Australian Institute of Health and Welfare (AIHW). Indigenous peoples make up around 2.5 percent of Australia's total population and are comprised of two separate groups, Australian Aborigines (90 percent) and people from the Torres Strait Islands (10 percent) (AIHW 2011a). The limited availability of policy-relevant Indigenous data was identified as a significant problem by the 1991 Royal Commission into Aboriginal Deaths in Custody (RCIADIC 1991). In partial response the AIHW now produces a biennial report, *The Health and Welfare of Australia's Aboriginal and Torres Strait Islander People*. As a further response, the federal government commissioned the 1994 *National Aboriginal and Torres Strait Islander Survey* (NATSIS): the first Australian national specific Indigenous data collection exercise, and additional NATSIS data collections have occurred in 2002 and 2008 (with another due in 2014).

In more recent years, as the "Closing the Gap" policy direction has gained momentum, there have been increasing demands for Indigenous population statistics to satisfy the emergent "evidence based" policy dictum. From 2008

Table 1.1: Australian National Demographic and Socio-Economic Comparison: Indigenous and Non-Indigenous Population

	Indigenous %	Non-Indigenous %
Proportion of the population	2.5	97.5
Aged 0–14 years	37	19
Aged 50 years +	11	31
School retention rate to Year 12	47	79
Aged 25-34 years and completed Year 12	30	73
Labor force participation	65	79
Home owners or purchasers	32	66
Live in overcrowded conditions	25	4
Rate of diabetes (age standardized)	12	4

Source: Statistics drawn from AIHW (2011a)

the Australian Prime Minister has given an annual Closing the Gap report to Parliament, outlining how its policies are being implemented and presenting statistical analyses of their results so far. Yet, despite the increasing focus, the evidence to date merely confirms that apart from small changes and largely short term, incremental changes, Aboriginals and Torres Strait Islanders remain firmly embedded at the bottom of every socio-economic indicator, as shown in Table 1.1.

In addition, our mortality and morbidity rates also stand out for all the wrong reasons: we are likely to die eleven years before our non-Indigenous counterparts; we retain much higher rates of infant mortality and lower birth weights. Adding to this somber picture are the data indicating that we are imprisoned at about seventeen times the rate of non-Indigenous Australians (AIHW 2011a; Walter 2008). Moreover, while the majority of our Aboriginal or Torres Strait Islander population is urban and only around one quarter of our population resides in remote locations, we share a common low socio-economic position. Poverty may be more visible in our remote communities, but remains the predominant material state of Australian Indigenous peoples regardless of where we live.

Regardless of the lack of progress in closing the gap, the policy response is more of the same: more behavioral intervention to address perceived Aboriginal deficits. For example, the non-attendance of children at school can now lead to their parents' welfare payments being suspended (Gordon 2011). This is not to suggest that such tough love policies are not well intended—there is a genuine desire among politicians and policy makers to reduce the socio-economic disparity between non-Indigenous and Indigenous Australians; rather, the point is that with the nation-state only being able to see Aboriginal and Torres Strait Islander people as in deficit, Indigenous policy also can only be seen through the lens of changing the Indigene to be more "normal."

Increasingly, the lack of policy success is also being linked to Indigenous behavioral deficits. In interviews relating to "Closing the Gap: Prime Minister's Report 2013," Australian Prime Minister Julia Gillard admitted that Indigenous children's literacy and numeracy results had not improved, and may have in fact worsened, since the previous year. She immediately followed this admission with the comment: "I have real fears that the rivers of grog that wreak [havoc] [sic] among Indigenous communities are starting to flow once again" (Woodley 2013: 1). The juxtaposition is very telling in what it did not say. She did not point out that the literacy and numeracy results applied across the nation but that the alcohol laws to which she was obliquely referring only applied to one small state.

What do these dire statistical pictures mean? We think Māori scholar Hokowhitu's (2009) concept of the "Indigeneity of immediacy" can help us think outside the dominant discourses that mark much of the debate in statistical discussions of Indigeneity. Hokowhitu's (2009) argument takes as its central axiom the importance of emphasizing "indigenous extentialism." Originally presented as a critique of Indigenous studies, his argument is that the field has been mired in a focus "around either the purity of a mythical pre-colonial past and/or 'decolonisation'. Meaning, [it] is largely divorced from the *immediacy* of the Indigenous condition" (2009: 101, emphasis in original). He suggests that the "colonial ghosts" that continue to haunt Indigenous studies' hunt for purity in the past must be excised to avoid the universalizing primitive/civilized discourses which lie at the heart of colonial constructions of Indigeneity.

Though perhaps not immediately obvious, Hokowhitu's broad approach to Indigeneity is useful to our critique of dominant statistical constructions of Aboriginality. That is, "savage constructions of Indigenous people" (2009: 101) sit as a dominant discourse at the heart of the larger projects of modernity that anchor colonizer settler nation-states' approaches to dealing with Indigenous peoples. It permits certain ways of talking about Indigeneity, while marginalizing others. Hokowhitu's (2009) argument also has a deep resonance for thinking about the kinds of knowledge construction that characterize Indigenous statistical research. It helps us to explore and delineate the paradigm of Indigenous quantitative methodologies.

Using Hokowhitu's lens of Indigenous immediacy, therefore, we perceive the current state of Indigenous statistics to mean two things. First, although he is talking specifically in the context of the "authenticity/ inauthenticity" debates characterizing Indigenous studies, his observations help to more broadly situate the power of dominant discourses to shape boundaries about which statements seem reasonable or useful in an Indigenous context and which are seen as divisive, irresponsible, or even nonsensical. Indeed, we can quickly see the extent to which development-based discourses, backed by a multiplicity of "objective" statistical data detailing the socio-economic depression of Indigenous communities (see Salée 2006 for an in-depth discussion of the Canadian literature), complicate our ability to demonstrate the value of such data to our communities beyond existing configurations. So the story (one with which we are in partial agreement) goes: the problems experienced by many of our Indigenous communities are real and longstanding (in relative terms), and as such, need solid information to be addressed and alleviated.

Closely following from a landscape sitting so squarely in the light of these development discourses—and in many ways more concerning than the issue of a lack of uptake in the Indigenous scholars' community—is how profoundly these discourses have shaped the manner in which policy makers and data collectors produce information about them. In our own research, we see the extent to which the very categories used to collect statistical information profoundly shape the kinds of interpretations possible, regardless of the technical accuracy of the statistical analyses themselves. Indeed, statistical experts spend far more time perfecting the technical flaws in their techniques and "cleaning" the data than they do exploring the interpretive limits of the very categories from which they draw their information. Even existing data are rarely analyzed in a manner that sits outside existing policy discussions. Indeed, in their defense, it would quite literally be a waste of public money to do so.

Our point is not to critique existing quantitative data for its technical deficiencies or inaccuracies. Instead, and more complexly, our point is that government policy makers (and for that matter, many Indigenous knowledge scholars, too) miss important elements of contemporary Indigenous sociality when they conceive of it *only* in the context of developmentally derived categories of analysis, *or*, in the spirit of resistance to this categorization, when they position Indigeneity in a manner that fails to account for our place in the everyday life of modern nation-states. In the context of contemporary Aboriginal policy making in Canada, Salée (2006: 5) asks: "Have the right questions been posed? Have all the issues been looked at? Have all the policy implications been examined? Has every angle of analysis been considered? Have the appropriate policies been proposed?" The answers to many of these kinds of questions rely on statistical information, so the same questions must be asked of the categories that shape those statistics and the "objective evidence" upon which policy claims about Indigenous communities are made.

Indigenous Statistics, Canadian Style

The Switch from Ethnicity to "Self-identification" in the Canadian Census

By definition, statistical fields like those of official census organizations are local to their national context. For more than a century and until recently, Statistics Canada (which collects Canada's census data) had been considered among the world leaders for quality of data, transparency of collection techniques, and broad collaboration with various groups and organizations in the "statistical cycle."[3] Canadian officials have been collecting "official" statistical information since 1871,[4] and until the 1980s had used ethnic ancestry as a primary basis for measuring the socio-cultural group differentiation (including Aboriginality) in Canada following successive policies that opened Canadian doors to waves of immigration during the late nineteenth and twentieth centuries.

The ethnicity literature underwent a transformation in the 1970s, however, from the idea that ethnicity is immutable and that we were born into it, to one that explored the varied contexts within which ethnicity is constructed and maintained through a mix of self-identification and community attachment (see Brubaker 2004 and Wimmer 2008 for a discussion of this literature). Not surprisingly, the broad changes in this literature were paralleled by longstanding discussions in the Canadian statistical field about how best to measure the socio-cultural variation among its population. Much of the early census administration divided humanity by *racial* designations, but by the end of WWII these had fallen out of vogue in favor of understanding it in terms of *ethnicity* (see Boyd et al. 2000; Walker 1997). Indeed, by 1951 all Canadian census references to race had been replaced by ethnic ancestry or origins questions. Both stressed the importance of commonality of descent or origins, but today ethnic ancestry or origins (rather than race) constitutes the principle category through which Statistics Canada measures socio-cultural variation in Canada (see Andersen 2013b).[5]

However, this issue assumes a particular form in the context of census measures of Aboriginality. It cannot be separated from its colonial context, either with respect to the racism that produced certain measures of Aboriginality, or in how it was counted in the census. Statistics Canada's information explains that although an ethnic origin question has been asked since 1871, it has undergone numerous changes with respect to the measurement of Aboriginality:

> Prior to 1951, Canada's Aboriginal people were defined by their tribal descent or their matrilineal descent (from the mother's side). This changed between 1951 and 1971 when Aboriginal people were defined by their patrilineal descent (from the father's side). From 1981 to the present, Aboriginal ancestry has been defined by descent from both the mother['s] and the father's side. In addition, since then, the ethnic origin question has allowed for the reporting of single and multiple responses. Prior to 1981, only single responses were permitted. (Statistics Canada 2010: 7)

It is important to understand, in a Canadian context, that the category of "Indian" sits at the administrative heart of more than a century of Canadian attempts to govern Aboriginal peoples, and as such, it has also served as the main category through which Aboriginal peoples were counted. Though "Indian" was defined legislatively in the mid-1850s, in 1876 an omnibus bill was created to incorporate previous pieces of legislation about the governance of Indigenous communities. This has become known as "The Indian Act." It has massively impacted the lives of Aboriginal individuals and communities who were defined as "status Indians" and who fell under its provisions. Likewise, it has shaped the kinds of social and legal relationships many Aboriginal peoples have been able to enter into with Canada (see Eberts 2010 and Palmater 2011 for a discussion of these issues).

However, even though the term "Indian" has maintained a longstanding presence, its legal and political meanings have undergone numerous changes, changes reflected in the census strategies for measuring it (and presented earlier in the Statistics Canada quote). Additionally, Curtis (2001), Hamilton (2007), Inwood and Hamilton (2011), and Ruppert (2009) have made it clear that the enumeration practices themselves took decades to stabilize as the saturation of official terms into Indigenous communities increasingly took hold alongside previous expressions of identity. Numerous difficulties plagued enumeration in these locales, in fact: basic problems included sharing a language; seasonably based, migratory lifestyles of Indigenous communities; geographical challenges of actually trekking into "remote" locations; legal and census definition conflicts; changing census categories (for example, in 1891, many Métis were recorded officially as French); differential access to confirmatory Department of Indian Affairs (DIA) band lists; following the so-called Riel Rebellion in 1885 (an Indigenous armed "insurrection"), increasingly fragile race relations that exacerbated already-existing suspicion about outside authorities; and Indigenous lifestyles (polygamy, different land tenures) that failed to fit existing census classifications (Hamilton 2007; Inwood and Hamilton 2010; Ruppert 2009).

In fact, census enumeration was considered so expensive, time consuming, and frustrating that census enumerations were often collected, second-order, through treaty lists and Indian Agents, and in other cases, through house-to-house visits (though these were thought to induce unnecessary excitement and speculation among enumeratees). Only when enumerations were otherwise unattainable did statistics officials distastefully rely on enumerations conducted by missionaries, explorers, and the Hudson's Bay Company. Indeed, in 1901 the census instructions explicitly extolled the virtues of employing Indian agents instead of census enumerators (Hamilton 2007: 65).

Despite these numerous changes in how information was collected and who collected it, "Indian" continues to represent the principle category through which Census Canada measured Aboriginal *ethnic ancestry* throughout much of the twentieth century. Its position—and what it was said to measure—apparently changed in the 1980s, however, when Statistics Canada officials underwent a change from more than a century of measuring Aboriginality by ethnic ancestry to measuring it via self-identification. Importantly, however, not just any self-identification: only a small number of categories of self-identification interested census enumerators, including "Inuit; Status or registered Indian; Non-status Indian; or Métis" (Statistics Canada 1981: 6).

This is somewhat confusing, not least because self-identification is usually positioned as an important element of ethnic ancestry: that is, ethnicity is the "subjectively felt sense of belonging based on the belief in shared culture and common ancestry" (Wimmer 2008: 973). Statistics Canada differentiates between ethnic ancestry and self-identification by defining the former in terms of a subjective sense of the ethnicity to which one's *ancestors* belonged (farther back than, say, one's grandparents) while defining the latter in terms of actual *self*-perception: that is, how one positions one's self in relation to that ancestry. Creating a divide between these two concepts, however, raises as many questions as it answers. How, for example, would this division allow for differentiating between differing *levels* of personal attachment to that feeling of ethnic origins or ancestry? Nonetheless, in 1986 Census Canada introduced the idea of "identity" to replace their origins/ancestry question. The new question asked: *"Do you consider yourself an Aboriginal person or a native Indian of North America that is, Inuit, North American Indian or Métis?"* to which respondents could answer *"No, I do not consider myself Inuit, North American Indian or Métis; Yes, Inuit; Yes, Status or Registered Indian; Yes, non-status Indian; or Yes, Métis"* (Statistics Canada 2010: 15).

The modification of census categories in the 1980s has today produced two principle estimates of Aboriginal population: the longstanding Aboriginal "ancestry" population, and a new "identity" population. With a size of about 1.7 million, the ancestry population is about 50 percent larger than the identity population, socio-economically much better off, and far more urban. Conversely, the identity population is much smaller (around 1.1 million), more socio-economically depressed, and more rural[6] in character. Given the kinds of policies government-sponsored data are used to support, Statistics Canada's switch to "identity population" data for its official presentation of the "Aboriginal population" is not surprising. Identity population characteristics are now broadly disseminated, both through Statistics Canada's publication series and through the "public use" data available to a wide array of data users. For all intents and purposes, it has become the primary population from which information is taken to shape policy on and intervention into Aboriginal communities in Canada. And, while ancestry estimates are still published, comparatively few policy actors make use of their information in relation to the identity data.

In a moment we will detail several problems with assuming that the move from ethnicity to self-identification indicates what we might think it does, as well as what it marginalizes. First, however, it is important to get some sense of the social context within which the "new" population began to gain in legitimacy following this switch. The split took place in the early 1980s during the lead up to (and immediately following) broad public consultations regarding possible changes to Canada's Constitution. In interviews with Statistics Canada officials undertaken by one of the authors, one informant explained that an Aboriginal organizational leader was dissatisfied with the ethnic ancestry question, believing that it failed to adequately capture the true character of Aboriginal identity. This leader asked for the addition of a self-identification question to be distributed to every Canadian household (as opposed to one in five as per the previous long form questionnaire schedule).

Analysis of these new data revealed stark differences in the population parameters of the "ancestry population" (whose members indicated only Aboriginal ancestry) and those who, in addition to indicating ancestry, also self-identified according to one (or more) of the government categories listed. As noted earlier, the identity population numbers were smaller, tended to live in rural areas, and were more socio-economically depressed. From an efficiency standpoint, it thus made far more sense to target the more developmentally lagged identity population than the larger but apparently better off (from a socio-demographic standpoint) ancestry population. Indeed, when asked why Statistics Canada made the switch from ethnicity to self-identification permanent, one Statistics Canada research participant concurred that this was most probably the case (see Andersen in press).

While the identity population has come to represent the base of virtually all analyzed and publicly disseminated data on Aboriginal people in Canada, important questions remain about what the switch actually means epistemologically and what it might indicate in terms of our understandings of identity. In a forthcoming article, Andersen (in press) explains these issues in further detail. He argues that on the one hand, most of us can easily discern between ancestry and self-identification in light of the fact that we probably know many people who have an Indigenous ancestor or two in their background but feel no day-to-day resonance. Surely, many might legitimately ask if this type of respondent can be differentiated from one with feelings of affiliation that rise to a level beyond that of historical curiosity? By definition, isn't someone who *self-identifies* as Aboriginal more legitimately Indigenous than someone who does not? Equally importantly from a policy perspective, aren't we more interested in the socio-demographic characteristics of respondents who self-identify as Aboriginal than those who (apparently) do not?

If it isn't obvious by now, our argument is that the issue is more complex than the way it is glossed over by most statisticians and policy makers. So let us begin by pulling at a puzzling string that statistical analysis cannot help us with (since by the time the data arrive for cleaning and analysis, it is too late to ask such interpretative questions): how do we go about differentiating between self-identification and ethnic ancestry and what did Statistics Canada think was the difference when they switched from the one to the other, *especially* given that the first census after the switch used the same categories to measure self-identification as had previously used to measure ancestry (see Kerr et al. 2003: 2–3)? Clearly, despite Statistics Canada's suggestion that this switch was monumental, the "new" self-identification data they derived were created using the same questions as they used to create previous data based on ethnic ancestry but with more specific administratively prescriptive answer categories.

However, this is not meant as a gotcha moment. The point of our discussion is not to "out" Statistics Canada for painting a switch from ethnic ancestry to self-identification that did not occur. Instead, our argument is that the categorical horizons of self-identification they switched to—that is, what came to *count* as Aboriginal self-identification—were narrowed according to developmentally based policy priorities in powerful but largely invisible ways (see Andersen in press). Little of this is critically examined with respect to thinking about the complex contexts within which this "policy population" gets naturalized as an "identity" population, nor does it assist us in thinking more broadly about what alternative—and arguably equally legitimate—identity populations might look like, ones more attentive to an Indigeneity of immediacy as detailed earlier by Hokowhitu (2009).

Aboriginal identity population estimates, shorn of this historical and contextual complexity, thus offer legitimate but predictable results. Within such narrow parameters of statistical configurations, it is little wonder that Canadian officials can speak so confidently about the(ir) statistical picture of the social conditions of Canada's Aboriginal communities and, in particular, the extent to which these communities lag behind those of the rest of Canada. Daniel Salée (2006: 5) writes that policy makers appear to possess

> a fairly good sense of what ails Aboriginal communities and individuals: the higher incidence of family violence, youth suicide, psychological distress and substance abuse, poorer individual health, weak or undeveloped capacity for economic development, the greater likelihood of exclusion from key labour markets, substandard housing and sanitary conditions—all of which makes life for them, at least on the surface, more difficult and less appealing.

It would be surprising if existing census classifications produced data on anything *but* these kinds of conditions. Not because they are not legitimately afflicting our communities but, rather, because current statistical configurations are *only* geared to produce empirical pictures of such conditions.

Indigenous Statistics, Australian Style

The Australian story of Indigenous statistics is a fraught one. Until amended by referendum in 1967, Section 127 of the Australian Constitution specifically excluded the "aboriginal race" from official population figures (Chesterman and Galligan 1997). The colonial assumption that Australian Aborigines were a "dying race" combined with concern that those states where larger numbers of Aboriginal people survived, by virtue of later colonizations, only claimed resources based on their Euro-Australian citizenry (Attwood and Markus 1999). Indigenous people were included in the national census from 1971. In 1995 the ABS formally adopted the following racial origin question as the standard for identifying persons as members of the Indigenous population: "*Are you of Aboriginal or Torres Strait Islander origin?* For persons of both Aboriginal and Torres Strait Islander origin please mark both 'Yes' boxes. Response options are: No; Yes, Aboriginal; and Yes, Torres Strait Islander" (ABS 2010). In this section we argue that while the direct racial discrimination of omission from previous censuses is remediated, the vestiges of the racialized presumptions that underpinned them remain.

Our argument that racialized presumptions remain embedded in official Indigenous statistics in Australia is centered around the political realities in which Indigenous statistics reside. As Zuberi and Bonilla-Silva (2008: 7) note, data do not tell a story in themselves. Rather, "we use data to craft a story that comports with our understanding of the world." The first Indigenous statistical "story" influence is that in the 2010s, despite the addition of statistical collections such as the National Aboriginal and Torres Strait Islander Survey (NATSIS), the five-year national censuses remain the main official source of data on Indigenous Australia. As noted above, Aboriginal and Torres Strait Islander people were not included in official census counts until 1971, and then, as now, Indigenous data were primarily generated by the inclusion of an Indigenous identifier question (Altman and Taylor 1996: 193). That is, they are an add-on, collected and collated according to the national count priorities already established for non-Indigenous Australia.

Secondly, and more compellingly for our argument, the "and Indigenous people" approach to data collection is that the apparatus of the nation-state is both the primary generator and the primary user of Indigenous statistical data. In a circular process, Australian state and federal government departments and authorities not only design, interpret, and disseminate nearly all Indigenous statistical data, they are also the predominant users and commissioners of these data. Indigenous statistics are fundamentally an Indigenous free zone with Indigenous peoples firmly the object of the research. While official data collection agencies such as the ABS laud their "engagement" with Indigenous people, this engagement is deeply circumscribed. For example, the ABS reports its consultations with its Advisory Group on Aboriginal and Torres Strait Islander Statistics (AGATSIS), a group drawn from commonwealth, state, and territory agencies, Indigenous peak bodies (associations of groups with allied interests), and data working groups (ABS 2007). Engagement, however, is not a "doing word," and it is clear from ABS reports that Indigenous presence within the action part on the purposive commissioning, analysis, interpretation, and use of the data is both limited and beholden.

We argue further that this circumscription is not neutral. Rather, the veiled but definite demarcation lines about the Indigenous presence in statistical space reveal the political and racial position from which Australian Indigenous data emanate. More significantly, they reveal that the dominant position in the realm that controls, commissions, analyses, and interprets Indigenous data is occupied by a group who constitutively share a social, racial, and economic position: middle class Euro-Australian. The result is a (mostly) subconscious shaping and restriction of Indigenous statistical portrayals, confining and/or prescribing how Indigenous data are conceived.

The social, economic, and racial distance of those producing data from the object of the data, Indigenous peoples, reinforces a largely uncontested, in Bourdieu's (1984) terms, a "synthetic unity" of dominant perspectives. Their underpinning ontology is clear in their genesis, practice, and interpretation. Within this worldview the Euro-Australian is the (unacknowledged) norm and the consistent Indigenous failure against these normed standards across multiple measures is deemed the problematic. The ontological frame is a presumption of pejorative Indigenous racial/cultural difference and a norm of Indigenous deficit. The discourse underpinning this ontological frame is common across the colonizer settler world and variously theorized as the deficit model along the lines of the culture of poverty thesis (Lewis 1966), or the poverty of Indigenous culture thesis (Sutton 2009). Within these theses, the common explanatory for statistical socio-economic differences between cultural sub-groups and the majority are posited as the values, behaviors, attitudes, and capacities of the "underperforming" group—in this case, Indigenous peoples. The questions generated from this ontological frame are "what" questions. They seek to establish/ re-establish the degree of that "what" via a constant probing of measures of the deep social, health, and economic inequalities that plague Indigenous peoples.

From an Indigenous ontology the more important question is not what differences exist, but why? A reversing of the ontological lens would compel different questions in a different research agenda. Yes, there are strong similarities in the social deprivation and marginalization of colonized Indigenous peoples in first world nations. Yet, culturally and experientially, our major similarity is our dispossession and subjugation by Anglo colonizers. Is this the central explanatory facet? Should the research agenda focus on probing the dimensions of white colonizer settler privilege to identify how societal resources and opportunities can be shared more equally? Such questions are more than just the inverse of questions related to Indigenous disadvantage. They resituate the problematic from the "deficit" Indigene to ask how the processes of colonization remain inextricably entwined on contemporary patterns of settler privilege. They also bring into the examination the concepts outlined earlier of liberal Western thought, civilized society, and how these are operationalized in contemporary settler states to embed and sustain race and culture aligned inequalities.

The overtly benign evidence base of Indigenous statistics, therefore, we argue, is methodologically embedded within a dominant middle class, colonizer settler ontological, epistemological, and axiological frame. Not surprisingly, it produces data that conform to its underpinning assumptions, values, and ways of understanding Indigenous reality. In the next section we use two examples to demonstrate how the dominant quantitative methodology of how Australian Indigenous statistics are done shapes the emergent statistical picture.

Simple Presentations, Difficult Interpretations

For State and Federal Government departments and authorities, the primary producers and consumers of Indigenous statistics, the criticality of Indigenous data has risen with the evidence base prerequisites for determining Closing the Gap policy directions. The disparate socio-economic position of Indigenous people is deemed so urgent that progress on closing the gap must be reported annually to Federal Government. The fifth prime minister Closing the Gap speech was made to the Australian Federal on February 6, 2013 (Closing the Gap 2013). There is, therefore, an increasing imperative as time since policy implementation elapses for data to indicate not only demographic and socio-economic patterning, but a (positive) change in that patterning. The polity of the Closing the Gap policy direction is a neo-liberal project with its focus on applying market solutions to Indigenous social and economic arenas (Walter 2009). Implicit in this frame is the individual as the object of enquiry. Yet, within the individualized focus, the racial demarcation remains undisturbed. The Indigene is a raced individual, and the statistical evidence on the position of these raced individuals is political territory.

The Indigenous statistical yardstick by which policy success, or lack of success, of measures such as Closing the Gap are publicly reported tend very strongly toward simple comparison and limited interpretations. The primary Indigenous statistical publication, *The Health and Welfare of Australia's Aboriginal and Torres Strait Islander People*, provides an example of how such presentations operate to entrench the position of the Indigene as deficit and to underplay the lack of policy outcomes. For example, the 2008 publication reports the Indigenous unemployment rate decreased (from 20 percent to 16 percent) between 2001 and 2006, an absolute positive change, adding that the ratio of decline is similar to that of the non-Indigenous population. What the term "similar ratio" does not make clear is that the relative proportional change is negative; the gap increased. The non-Indigenous unemployment rate declined by around 29 percent, but the Indigenous rate, off a much higher base, declined by only 20 percent (Walter 2008). The 2011 publication, while noting that the halving of the gap in employment outcomes between Indigenous and non-Australians by 2018 is a key policy objective of governments, reports no direct comparison. Rather, it is just noted that "the unemployment rate for Indigenous Australians was higher than for non-Indigenous Australians across all age groups." This statement is accompanied by an aggregated bar chart with no percentage figures given and which compares Indigenous and non-Indigenous employment proportions to a total of 100 percent. The portions of the bars comprise the proportion of each group undertaking CDEP employment (the Commonwealth Development Employment Program is an Indigenous only "work for welfare payments" program), the proportion employed non-CDEP, the proportion unemployed, and the proportions of each population categorized as "Not in the Labour Force" (AIHW 2011a: 19). It is nigh on impossible to assess from this figure if the Indigenous/non-Indigenous unemployment gap is widening or closing. Given the highlighting of even marginal statistical improvements in other parts of the publication, we can only assume that the gap has widened.

Simple frequency counts also occlude vital aspects, such as the dramatically different demographic composition of the aggregate Indigenous population. The AIHW (2008) reports an increase, from 20 to 23 percent between 2001 and 2006, in the proportion of Indigenous people aged fifteen years and over who had completed Year 12 (the final year of secondary schooling in Australia)—a positive absolute change. Incorporating the very youthful profile of the Indigenous population into the analysis, and given that the vast majority of Year 12 completers are aged seventeen to nineteen provides a different interpretation. The higher proportion of the Indigenous population (more than double) in this age range means Indigenous Year 12 achievement rates should be rising faster than in the older non-Indigenous population (Jackson 2008). But it is not. In relative terms, the ratio of non-Indigenous to Indigenous Year 12 education achievement also rose (Walter 2010c). In the 2011 edition (AIHW 2011a), there is no comparative percentage reported for the proportional rates of Indigenous and non-Indigenous people holding a Year 12 achievement. There are data on retention rates from Year 7/8 (the start of Australian secondary schooling), with the text reporting that the 2010 Indigenous retention rate to Year 12 is 47 percent versus 79 percent for non-Indigenous school children. But while the text says that halving the school retention rate gap by 2020 is a government policy and that the retention rate has increased from 29 percent in 1996, there is no information provided on whether the relative retention rate gap is still declining. Again a hard to interpret graph suggests that the gap is not narrowing. The simplicity of the presentations belies the statistics' active existence as racially politicized objects. This is not a claim of ideological subjectivity. Instead, the purpose is to highlight the context in which data are produced and presented. While the overt intention is to disseminate a neutral statistical reflection of the Australian Indigenous social and economic reality, this perception fails to acknowledge that it is a particular view of reality being reflected. The difficulty of the data interpretation highlights the implications of these data. A simple, undemanding, but very difficult to interpret analysis keeps the focus on Indigenous people and culture, epistemologically situated as "the object problem," as Hokowhitu (2009) argues: a problem with problems. Covertly then, such statistical "results" prove that Indigenous peoples and culture are in deficit and both must be reshaped to remediate their lack of fit, axiologically and ontologically, into "normal" Australian society.

The Orthodoxy of the Dichotomy

While the process vagaries of simple presentations and difficult interpretations obscure policy outcomes while highlighting deficit, the practice of comparison is itself deeply political and methodology entrenched in the way Indigenous statistical data are done. The default analytical norm of Australian Indigenous data is their comparison with data from the non-Indigenous population. Yet, such methodological practice operates to place the Indigene as the Other before data are even examined (Walter 2010c). It is the Indigene compared to the rest in a way that allows the ordinariness of this dichotomized portrait to be infused by a subtle depreciatory tone.

The comparatively small Australian Indigenous population magnifies the dichotomizing pejorative effect. This statistical imbalance leads to the analytical and interpretive tendency to aggregate, via the broad category of the "Indigenous population." While conventionally categorized as one group for statistical purposes, Australian Indigenous peoples are by no means homogeneous, and significant demographic, social, and cultural differences exist within and across populations. Even the existing aggregations are a statistical convenience rather than a reflective picture. There are more than 500 Aboriginal and Torres Strait Islander nations, and before colonization more than 250 distinct languages were spoken. More than 145 are still spoken today (Office offor the Arts n.d.). Today, it is Indigenous peoples such Dharug, Noongar, Yorta Yorta, and Larrakia who make up Indigenous Australia. Each of these peoples has a unique history, a unique historical and contemporary affiliation to country and each also has a unique and living cultural identity, (Walter 2008; 2010c). State, geographically remote or urban disaggregation does occur, but usually only for limited variables. The outcome is a dichotomized, mostly nationally aggregate comparative norm that, while supporting statistical function, is an essentialist positioning. It disregards and nullifies, in both policy and Indigenous understanding terms, the diversified identity and reality of Aboriginal and Torres Strait Islander Australia. It also decontextualizes the dire picture of embedded social, economic, political, and cultural inequality that the data represent from the places and spaces where this inequality is taking place on a daily basis.

Figure 1.1 and Table 1.1 presented earlier in this chapter are examples of how Indigenous data are commonly presented in both Australia and Canada. And as argued earlier, the "what" and "how" of the comparisons and the methodological presumptions shaping how these comparisons are conceived and interpreted also shape our understanding of their apparent "reality." Our central argument is that simple comparisons are not race neutral statistical displays. Dichotomizing and framing Indigenous data using Euro-Australian defined studies, variables, priorities, and interpretations is not the only, or the best, way to use Indigenous data (see Walter 2008; Taylor 2011).

More crucially, the norm of the dichotomous analysis, in its apparently benign presentation, still reflects the differential social space positioning of the object and subject. The acquired and subjective natures of established approaches are shielded by the ordinariness (and narrowness) of existing Indigenous data traditions. That is, in established practices using Indigenous data the analysis and interpretation are so normalized that they belie their foundational methodology—which, since colonization, has been that of the Euro-Australian majority. The social positioning of the non-Indigenous "owners" of data flows into their interpretation without conscious intent, but with substantive and often predictable outcomes. As argued by Atkinson, Taylor, and Walter (2010: 328), "rooted in the hermetic boundedness and power asymmetries inherent in the shared position of their producers, Australian Indigenous data 'stories' are unlikely to deviate from well-worn, themes of disadvantage and deviation."

Finally, in some cases a lack of comparative data can also serve to highlight Indigenous deficit. In the 2011 *The Health and Welfare of Australia's Aboriginal and Torres Strait Islander People* data on the proportion of the heavy disease burden of the Indigenous population caused by eleven selected health determinants are cited. Labelled in the heading as "risky health behaviours" (AIHW 2011a: 36), 12 percent of the burden is attributed to smoking; 11 percent and 8 percent to obesity and inactivity respectively; alcohol, 5 percent; low fruit and vegetable consumption, 3 percent; and 1 percent for risky sexual behavior. There are no comparative data of disease burden related to "risky behaviour" among the non-Indigenous population, nor is there any attempt to place these factors in any socio-structural context of poverty, marginalization, or limited and neglected social and health infrastructure.

Conclusion

This chapter has focused on the ways in which officially conceived data like that produced through the census create technically accurate but narrowly conceived statistical configurations of Aboriginal sociality in Canada and Australia and, more specifically, how deeply such statistical stories are indebted to development-based models of policy. Moreover, the categories of "identity" to which the various indicators of socio-demographic status are cross-tabulated constrict or limit our "statistical imagination" in ways unhelpful for thinking more broadly about who our communities are, statistically, and what can be measured that is not. In Canada, the switch from ethnic ancestry to self-identification is really a switch from non-policy-relevant ethnic identification to policy-relevant identification. Thus, in a very real way current dominant trends in Aboriginal statistics are marginalizing alternative (and in many cases, more positive) stories about Aboriginality that sit in stark contrast to the stories told using official data. Unmasking the unspoken methodological approach to Indigenous data production allows their usual "straightforward" comparative presentation in national data to be seen within the political and racial terrain of their origins.

Notes

1   In this book we define racialization as the "processes through which certain physical and cultural differences are emphasized, elevated, and distinguished between such that races are produced and legitimized" (Andersen 2011: 57).

2   Highlights from the Royal Commission on Aboriginal peoples. www.aadnc-aandc.gc.ca/eng/1100100014597 (accessed March 1, 2012).

3   We use the term "the statistical cycle" here to help us think in terms of the creation, collection, analysis, dissemination, and policy use of census information, from start to finish, for each five year cycle between (Canadian) censuses. Importantly, the cycle is also comprised of a series of interpretive decisions that ultimately shape what follows it, in that cycle and in future cycles.

4   1871 is considered the first "scientific" census. Large-scale census collection had occurred prior to that but was considered unreliable for various reasons (see Curtis 2001 for a fascinating and in-depth discussion of the dynamics of historical data collection in Canada).

5   This was augmented by the addition of an arguably more biologically deterministic "visible minority" question in 1996.

6   In Canada, many Aboriginal communities are contained within administrative "reserve" locales that are largely situated in rural areas. Such reserves have been in place for more than a century and have retarded the growth of the urban Aboriginal population in Canada (which is why the current proportion of the Aboriginal population that is urban—slightly more than 50 percent—is so low compared to virtually every other country that counts an Aboriginal population). Administratively, the federal government only admitted responsibility for "Indians living on reserve lands," greatly impacting the ways in which urban Aboriginal policymaking has been undertaken (see Andersen and Strachan 2012).

Chapter 2

Conceptualizing Quantitative Methodologies

Introduction

What is a methodology? How do we recognize one when we see it and how do we determine what sort of methodology it is? Equally importantly, what makes it Indigenous? These seem like straightforward enough questions, but they are surprisingly hard to answer using research tomes as your sources. Yet these questions must be both asked and answered as a first step in articulating an Indigenous quantitative methodology. Only when we understand what constitutes a methodology can we differentiate *Indigenous* quantitative methodologies from other kinds.

Within the whitestream academy, clearly explaining to our students what a methodology is—as well as how it differs from a method—has always been fraught. *Method*, of course, is relatively straightforward in its definition as a technique for gathering and analyzing information, such as a survey or content analysis. *Methodology* is a different matter. Our experience with research books and texts is that they either avoid the problem by not defining methodology at all (for example, see Bryman 2004; Denzin and Lincoln 2008; Matthews and Ross 2010; Neumann 2004) or provide only very limited definitions. In their text on research methods in politics, for example, Burnham et al. (2004: 4) define methodology as "a study of the principles and theories which guide the choice of method." The best selling US text, *The Practice of Social Research* (Babbie 2007: 4), mentions methodology only once, stating, "*Epistemology* is the science of knowing: *methodology* (a subfield of epistemology) might be called the science of finding out." In a similar vein, Maxim (1999) terms methodology as the approach or philosophy of how we study social phenomena.

Indigenous Statistics: A Quantitative Research Methodology by Maggie Walter and Chris Andersen, 41–57. © 2013 Left Coast Press, Inc. All rights reserved.

Our own early definition of methodology (see Walter 2006) was slightly more expansive than these. It positioned methodology as the theoretical lens or worldview through which research is understood, designed, and conducted. This definition, which added the concept of worldview, was arguably more useful than those cited above, but only just. At least one bright student each semester asks what exactly is included in this lens and, more particularly, how can the data it brings into focus be recognized, described, and conceptualized in research? Our search through available resources found no clear-cut responses to these excellent and flummoxing questions. So we also tended to obfuscate, just repeating the worldview explanation in different words.

Students were never really satisfied, and neither were we. Our desire to more clearly articulate methodology's meaning(s) was further piqued and clouded by the other scholarly attempts to delineate at least some of the aspects of what 'worldview' might mean within methodologies. For example, many feminist methodologies include a reflexive component, an open acknowledgment of the power and the presence of researchers in the field. This reflexivity tends to sit alongside the more specific recognition of the previously unacknowledged importance of gender in how research is conceptualized and practiced. Other fields, such as hermeneutics, epistemically recognize that understandings of truth and reality are created socially via a process of constantly evolving interpretive frameworks (Ezzy 2002). Participatory Action Research and Critical Discourse Analysis also build in aspects of their methodological lens by making their value systems explicit. Participatory Action Research, for example, centers the ownership and control of the research enquiry, process, and practice with the community that is the subject of the research problem; the researcher is considered the facilitator (Walter 2010b). Critical Discourse Analysis places the importance of accounting for power and its deployment at the heart of its research practice and disavows the possibility of objectivity within any research method (Jacobs 2010).

A few methodological tracts do define aspects of their epistemological framing, but they are exceptions that prove the rule and highlight the absence of this practice within these debates more generally. Nowhere is this more evident than in research that uses quantitative methodology. While the vast majority of quantitative social researchers now strongly resist the positivist label, the positivist framework has not been explicitly replaced; it seems to have merely been discarded. This consensus has produced a ubiquity of quantitative methodology that seemingly requires no further explanation. Its primary methodological point of reference is reduced to its differences from qualitative methodologies. The problem with such ubiquity is that the methodological practice of such quantitative research failed, and fails, to recognize its own culturally and racially situated origins and, more particularly, its contemporary dominant cultural and racial parameters. By emphasizing racial and cultural parameters we are overtly recognizing that the majority of its practitioners are racially white and from European or Euro-colonizer origins—and that these origins not only shape but vastly narrow the methodological cultural assumptions under which research is conducted and analyzed. We suggest, further, that these methodological prescriptions prevent the clear conceptualization of a non-positivist quantitative methodology. More specifically, a conceptualization of quantitative methodology for researchers of Indigenous topics in the first world nations where colonized Indigenous peoples now live does not seem to exist.

Our dissatisfaction with methodology was amplified when we began trying to understand how our own work could be categorized as Indigenous quantitative methodology. How could we define our research practice as a distinctly Indigenous quantitative methodology if we did not first delineate, in a concrete way, our employment of the term? We also noted that students and scholars (often of European descent), on hearing us present our work, would ask how our methodology differed from theirs. In response, we asked them to articulate exactly which aspects of standard quantitative methodologies they wanted us to contrast Indigenous methodology with. That is to say, we attempted to turn the telescope around, to get them to denaturalize their own methodologies and to think about them as something other than "the norm," with which Indigenous methodologies should then be contrasted.

Most were unable to name any specifics, perhaps just commenting distractedly and imprecisely about "approach." We then asked them to outline their own approach so we could clarify where the differences lay. You can see where the circulatory pattern of this question and answer session usually ended up: nowhere. What intrigued us about such questioning was not that our audience wanted to know how an Indigenous quantitative methodology differed from other methodologies, but that they wanted us to provide a coherent picture of our methodologies when they could not provide a coherent picture of theirs. Though we thought we knew what an Indigenous quantitative methodology was, we realized that answers based around the principles and philosophical tenets that underpin Indigenous methodologies were not enough. We needed to define a more generic methodology before we could define an Indigenous quantitative methodology.

Our thinking started with the ambiguities of our own field, social science. As teachers we emphasize to students the scientific, methodical aspects of research practice, the need for clarity of purpose, transparency of approach, and rigor of method and objectivity in analysis and interpretation. However, we also stress that the practice of social research is not a neutral endeavor. No research is "objective" if by objective one means standing outside of social power. For if research is truly impartial, how can we explain why we prioritize some social research projects over others or why some questions are asked, but not others? And how is it that different researchers interpret the same data so differently? Our methodology, we realized, is at least in part an explanation of this complex terrain. We also realized that being Indigenous researchers gave us special insight into the fraught task of conceptualizing the dimensions of a methodology when geared toward Aboriginal issues.

The understandings we bring to research thus incorporate, up front, important elements that usually remain unstated and unacknowledged within Western methodologies. That is, as Indigenous researchers, it is incumbent upon us not only to approach our research from the position of Indigenous people as the knowers rather than as merely the subjects of Indigenous society, but also to declare who we are as researchers and why the research question we are asking and answering is important—not only for our academic discipline, but also to us as individuals and, relationally, as members of our respective peoples. According to the old standby definition of a methodology as the lens through which the research is approached, we were already directly addressing at least some of the facets of this lens.

A Recipe for Methodology

When Sonia Maria Sotomayor, a United States federal judge of Puerto Rican descent who was raised in a South Bronx tenement by a single mother, was nominated to the Supreme Court, a debate exploded about whether her cultural and socioeconomic background would influence her interpretation of the constitution. By contrast, the same debate did not exist when John Roberts—a Caucasian from Indiana with an "American as apple pie" background—was nominated for the court. Only "the other" is cultural and thus incapable of impartiality. The same phenomenon exists in academia: the question of how culture, race, gender, and socioeconomic background affect research methodology tends to arise only when the researcher is seen as somehow "other" and not when the researcher is part of the "unmarked," dominant norm.

It is critical, however, to insist that these considerations are central to all methodology. Figure 2.1 shows our conceptualization of methodology in three components: standpoint, theoretical frame, and methods. These elements are inextricably entwined in practice, but it is helpful to clarify each ingredient separately. We emphasize that we are providing an overarching definition of what a methodology is—a starting point that underpins all methodologies, not just Indigenous or just traditional Western methodologies. In this section we have chosen specifically not to use Indigenous examples in order to keep the reader's attention on how *all* methodology is comprised of these three elements, not just the methodologies used by those positioned as "the other," such as Indigenous peoples.

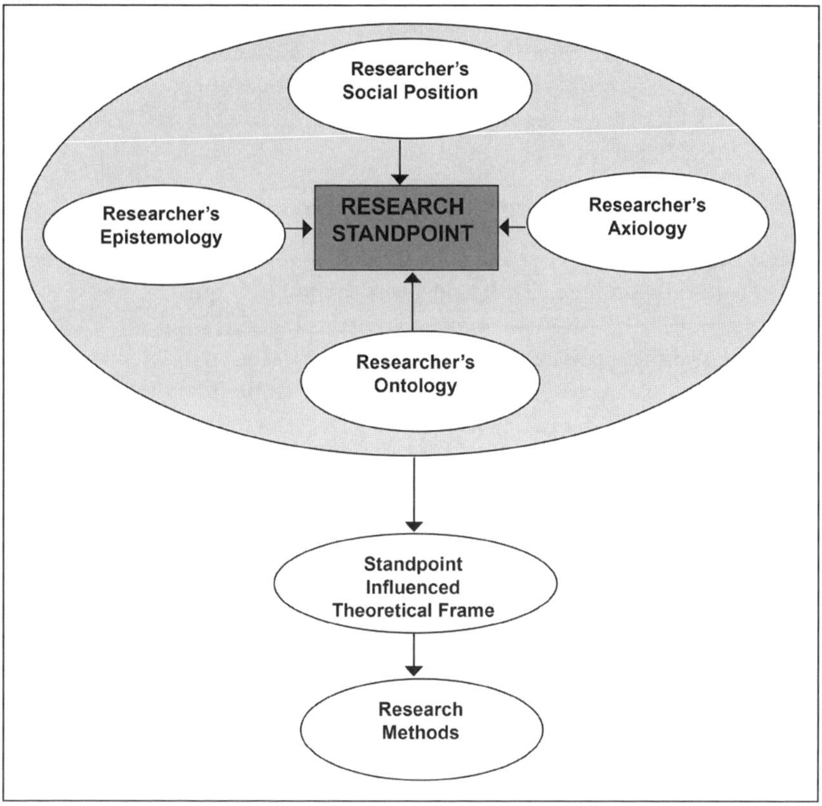

Figure 2.1: Conceptualization of a Research Methodology

This understanding and the deliberate attempt to denaturalize what we might otherwise take for granted allow us to identify and explicitly declare facets of a methodology. Who we are, the values that underpin our concept of self, our perspectives on the world and our own position within it, our realities, and our understandings of how knowledge is construed and constructed are each part of the complex puzzle involved in exploring the underpinnings of methodology. As a component of methodology, we summarize this set of facets as our *research standpoint*. Research standpoint is arguably the most important determinant of a research project's methodology. It pre-exists and fundamentally influences our choices of theoretical frame and method. Most critically, research standpoint is a fundamental component of *all* methodologies, not just Indigenous ones. Moreover, the failure to recognize one's standpoint in fact magnifies, rather than mitigates, its influence on research practice.

The term 'standpoint' has been used by other research methodology scholars, especially feminist scholars, but while acknowledging the theoretical debt to such work, we conceptualize the term differently. In our formulation, standpoint incorporates within it the philosophical tenets of *epistemology, axiology,* and *ontology* that have been central to the Indigenous methodological literature (which we discuss later in further detail), as well as *social position* (see Moreton-Robinson and Walter 2010).

Social Position

Our *social position* comprises and reflects much of who we are socially, economically, culturally, and racially. It underpins the research questions we see, the answers we seek, the way we go about seeking those answers, the interpretations we make, and the theoretical paradigms that make sense to us. Social position is an essential element of methodology because, as Bourdieu (1984) argued, it is this position in three dimensional social space—comprised of social, cultural, and economic capital—that creates the filters and frames through which we make sense of the world and our own position within it. We would add racial capital (see Walter 2010c) to Bourdieu's set and speak in terms of four-dimensional social space. Race is also a capital, the various values of which are reflected in the racial hierarchy of each society. First world settler nations have particular patterns of racial hierarchy. These reflect colonization and its processes of possession/dispossession, privilege/disprivilege, and entitlement/marginalization (Walter 2010c: 47). The descendants of the Anglo-colonizers occupy the top position, usually followed by others of Western European descent, followed in turn by various other migrant groups with hierarchical position largely dictated by the elapse of time since the major waves of their migration.

Also patterned is the position of the Indigenous peoples of those nations at, or near, the bottom of the hierarchy. A four-dimensional conception of social space, therefore, allows the recognition of the raced nature of social, cultural, and economic capital within our social position. Like social, cultural, and economic capital, race capital is deployed to competitively garner the societal goods, knowledge, status, services, and power relations that are produced and circulate as resources in societies. It is our position in social space, our capital relationalities, that shapes our life chances, and while we experience relationalities and life chances as individuals, we share this position with those of similar social, economic, cultural, *and* racial capitals. Social position not only substantially prescribes our life circumstances and experiences themselves, it also shapes the worldview through which we understand them.

Shining a light on the social, cultural, economic, and racial aspects of our personal identity as a crucial aspect of framing methodology helps us understand the ambiguous terrain of research practice. Our gender is central to how we understand ourselves and how society understands us, and as Pateman (1991) has made clear, in research gender shapes not only the questions we ask, but how we conceptualize the role of research itself. Similarly, our age, the times we were born into and have lived through, means that older and younger researchers are likely to see the social landscape of research in different terms (Howard et al. 2002). Race also matters. As Zuberi and Bonilla-Silva (2008) argue in the United States, African-American researchers tend to ask different questions than do White-American researchers (Zuberi and Bonilla-Silva 2008); Kerbo (1981) asks why most (predominantly middle class) social researchers tend to investigate topics that concentrate on poorer, less educated segments of the population, rather than their own class grouping.

Critically, social position is neither just about the individual or just about individual choices. A researcher can be consciously egalitarian, libertarian, non-sexist, and non-racist in his or her attitudes, but this does not nullify the impact of his or her class, culture, race, and gender on his or her worldview; not least because so much of it is taken for granted. Social position is, thus, a verb rather than a noun: we do, live, and embody social position, and as researchers, it covertly, overtly, actively, and continuously shapes how we do, live, and embody research practice. And as Bourdieu (1984) argues further, it marks us not only as individuals but as members of a group who share specific social, cultural, economic, and racial positions. Despite post-modernist emphasis on the fluidity of our own sense of identity, it is not possible to move completely away from the self that is indelibly marked by who we are socially, racially, culturally, and economically. The self is bounded. No matter how much we empathize and engage, we cannot *be* "the other" nor can we inhabit that social space, however much we think it is or wish it were so; we remain irretrievably our specifically located selves.

Equally crucially, it is this self that is reflected in our research practice. This is not to disparage empathy and active engagement. Both are vital to good research practice, no matter the social position of the researchers. They can and do result in genuine insight for the researcher (including Indigenous researchers) into the reality of the object group of the research. But they are an addition to, not a replacement for, the impact of the researcher's social position on his or her own research practice.

Epistemology

We can glimpse the impact of social position within the milieu of the next element, *epistemology*. Epistemology, the study of knowledge, is, of course, central to all research practice. Epistemology explores theories of knowledge or, more pragmatically, ways of knowing. Research, concerned with the generation of new knowledge, is at its core. Its epistemological base must also, therefore, be core to the "what" and "how" of that new knowledge. Yet, while traditional Western philosophy saw epistemology as outside of, or prior to, culture, what we regard as "knowledge" is in fact encapsulated within a social and cultural framework. Epistemological theory concerns itself with understanding how the (mostly unwritten) rules about what is counted as knowledge are set—what is defined as knowledge, who can and cannot be "knowledgeable," which "knowledges" are valued and, by extension, which are marginalized.

Epistemological reflexivity is typically absent from traditional Western methodologies, particularly quantitative ones. They have been the norm, and "normal" gets conflated with "natural." These methodologies contain within them the basic tenets of societally dominant ways of knowing, but like a fish in water, most researchers don't subject these ways of knowing to scrutiny. Sometimes, however, the fish unexpectedly finds itself out of water, and for research this is when the epistemological shapers of research become clear. For example, the United States Census used to employ official census takers who made home visits to count individuals and make demographic designations, such as race and ethnicity. When this practice was replaced by surveys and individuals self-reported their demographic data, the racial make-up of the United States changed radically. When civil servants made racial determinations, 40 percent of those with Puerto Rican background were designated as white/ Caucasian, whereas over 80 percent of these people self-reported as white when they had the chance to create their own demographic knowledge about themselves. Changing the identity of the knowers of racial identity from civil servants to the people themselves dramatically changed the results (Wade 2012).

Who was right? Western nations still debate whether racial identity is something that only scientists can know objectively, or a decision individuals make for themselves, or some complex combination of the two. This question of how to identify knowers, who can know, and how hierarchies of knowledges are constructed is critical for all research methodologies, not just Indigenous ones. But because the dominant society has refused to acknowledge Indigenous peoples as knowers, and historically seen them only as subjects of knowledge, Indigenous scholars are justifiably at pains to emphasize epistemology as an essential element of Indigenous methodologies.

Dominant epistemological research practices have, of course, not gone without critique. Many Indigenous scholars (see, for example, Moreton-Robinson 2004) and feminist scholars have challenged the assumed objectivity and rationality of dominant ways of designating and valuing knowledge. The central critique for feminists is how these research practices have ignored how the social relations of gender shape knowledge production and the value and validity of that ensuing knowledge. A feminist social epistemology challenges the abstract individualism of social theories and theorists. It points out the invisibility of what should otherwise be blindingly obvious—that until very recently these social, economic, psychological, and cultural theories (and many others besides) were essentially all produced by middle and upper class European or North American males. In contrast, Annie Oakley's (1974) groundbreaking thesis placed gendered knowledges at the center of her analysis to show how housework oppressed women via the emotionalization of menial, dirty, and unrewarded labor as "love and care" and, by default, an exclusively feminine activity. This scholarship acknowledges (and celebrates) gendered knowledge as a central aspect of its epistemological base. Oakley's work also illuminated the basic fact that knowledge production is framed by the attributes of the knowledge producer, that the epistemology within the methodology—*all* methodology—is culturally and socially positioned.

The experiential existence of knowers (researchers and scholars) therefore has epistemic consequences. The epistemology of methodology is about whose voices or knowledges are validated and prioritized, and perhaps even more decisively, whose are not. The epistemic core of research methodology is thus as much about absences as it is about presences. Critically, these presences and absences are not merely related to voices prioritized and validated within the data. The epistemic validation and prioritization, the presences and the absences, occur at each and every step of the research process, from conception to conclusion. Imperative to this understanding is the recognition that, even more than individual researchers or scholars who reflect a positional epistemology into their research methodology, social institutions—all institutions, really, but for our purposes especially universities—constitute central sites of knowledge production. As such, they reflect, maintain, and sustain dominant societal understandings of how knowers are and can be and the dominant way of organizing the hierarchy of both knowledges and the knowledge production itself.

To give one example of many regarding institutional constraints: quantitative research articles usually follow a reasonably rigid structure of presentation. The research problematic is introduced, the literature reviewed, followed by a discussion of the method, the data, their analysis, and discussion of the results, all of which require a certain format. Despite how natural or normal it feels for those who undertake their research dissemination using that form, both the knower and the data themselves are positioned within a specific epistemological context. For those living outside the Western methodological norm (that is, outside the university setting and without the training required to make this format seem rational), this format can be alien to their ways of knowing. To comply is to feel epistemologically straitjacketed, but to deviate from that format is to risk having the article rejected by reviewers.

Axiology

Axiology refers to the theory of *extrinsic and intrinsic values*, concepts that are palpably part of methodology, *all* methodology. Hard-line positivism is now passé within social and other population research, and few if any researchers in these fields still hold the view that research and researchers can and do produce value-neutral knowledge from the mere and objective observation of facts. The more contemporary question is to ask how a researcher's value systems and those of the groups and institutions associated with the research can be disentangled from their practice of research.

If we accept that regardless of intent, research can never exist in a value free zone, then we must also recognize values as an unavoidable feature of research practice. Further, these values will likely reflect the social position of the researcher and/or his or her institution or funding body. The reasoning we offer to support this claim is balanced on two key points. First, social and population research occurs in the social world, a world where moral, political, and cultural values are an integral, if largely invisible, facet of the social landscape. Therefore, research conducted within the social landscape must at least partly reflect the dominant mores of that landscape. Second, the formulated research topic or question brings with it its own social, cultural, political, and moral milieu. The topic cannot be extricated from its context without rendering it devoid of meaning (Walter 2010a).

Researchers can gain insight into their own axiological framework by asking themselves reflective, value-querying questions, like why are we interested in the research topic? The fact that funding was available is still reflective of values, because it still begs the question of why *that* one was chosen; why have we decided to focus on this specific aspect of the topic; how and why have we framed our research questions in the ways we have; how have we conceptualized our key concepts and why we have conceptualized them this way; how and why did we decide that this particular topic and/or question was worth researching as opposed to the uncountable others that could also be the subject of our research? The critical point is that the questions we ask and the research decisions we make are not spontaneous. They emerge from somewhere, and having emerged, are deemed by us as worthy of investigation.

When asked why a particular topic or question, most researchers will respond that it interests them. But what stimulates that interest? The answer is invariably interlaced with value statements. As embedded members of their society, researchers' questions reflect the moral, political, racial, and cultural values that guide and frame their research. To suggest, therefore, that our research is divorced from our personal and cultural values is patently not true. Yet, researchers frequently continue to make such claims, often calling upon their disciplinary professionalism as proof of their status as independent, objective scholars.

For example, MaryRose Casey (2008) showed how the race of European Australian academics has been deployed to protect white Australian virtue in current debates on what actually happened to Aboriginal peoples during colonization. White history academics, she argues, assumed the perspective of detached, disinterested subject to present and judge Australia's histories while simultaneously positioning Indigenous perspectives as non-rigorous and politicized. In Canada, this has taken the form of a recent attack by Widdowson and Howard (2008), who have argued that Indigenous society is less advanced on the human evolutionary scale in comparison to non-Indigenous Canadian society and, as such, any knowledge put forward by contemporary Indigenous communities toward (for example) the environment (that is, traditional ecological knowledge) must necessarily be reviewed as inferior and, as such, regarded with suspicion.

Importantly, the presumption of objectivity is rarely extended to Indigenous scholars or scholarship. At discipline-based conferences we are often confronted by audience comments that because our work frequently involves questioning accepted Western assumptions, it is political and, by inference, not "proper" research. When we respond by pointing out the political character of their work, which often reflects the very (dominant) assumptions we are querying, they are frequently outraged. It seems that, by default, our work can only be political, whereas their work, apparently unaffected by their racial and societal positioning, is, equally by default, rigorous, neutral, and objective. Our efforts to point to the value-laden genesis of such an assumption is usually met with incredulity and often dismissed as further proof of our own inability to exhibit the core researcher values of neutrality and objectivity. There is a conscious resistance to recognizing how race and culture are present in the work that settler scholars do, while at the same time Indigenous researchers are labelled as activists. As whiteness scholars argue, whiteness, and the privileges attached, usually remains invisible, unnamed, and unmarked, and this is how it preserves its privilege (see Bonilla-Silva 2010; Frankenberg 1993; Lipsitz 2006; Mills 1997; Moreton-Robinson 2008;Riggs 2004).

Acknowledging our axiological frame, of course, does not mean we should not aspire to ensure the trustworthiness of our analyses (if not necessarily an obsession with ensuring that the analyses are replicable). The research project relies on open and professional practice in which research rigor remains an essential element, regardless of the researcher's location in social space. Nevertheless, all researchers make choices within their research, and these choices not only have an integral values base, they also influence how the data are interpreted and presented, as shown in the previous chapter. Gaining insight into our own axiological frame and its position within our methodology, alongside the recognition that values are, implicitly at least, embedded in all research, allows us to read our own research and that of others reflexively, with an eye to the values informing it. More specifically, reflecting on the influence of particular values and on how we are approaching our research practice is not enough; we have to acknowledge those values within the research itself.

Ontology

Ontology is concerned with the nature of being and the categories that we use to make sense of social reality. An ontological frame refers to how people perceive and operationalize a conception of that reality; how they "be" within their social world; and the relationship among themselves, others, and the constitutive entities of that world. Like the other elements of standpoint, ontology tends to merit little discussion in research methodology debates, especially those of quantitative methodology. The primary reason for this, we argue, is that how people "be" is only seen as a legitimate question if those people or peoples are not of Euro-settler origin. The discourse of individualism eschews the concept that how we "are" in the world is a cultural construction. Instead, the focus is on how the individual "'is'" who he or she really is, with this special "you" expressed through his or her personal style—clothing, hair, friends, leisure activities.

Of course, it is not as simple as that. Actualities of one's sense of reality and of being are neither concrete nor immutable. Our experience of what is real and how we respond to that perceived reality can be fluid and, at times, contradictory. A home, for example, is just a dwelling that is designated as "home." But the *concept* of home still has a palpable existence, one that is liberally laced with emotional, psychological, cultural, social, and even economic realities that have very little to do with the physical shape and form of the house. Moreover, the reality of what constitutes home changes over time or by the viewer. The home may be the center of life for a young family, but to the engineer planning a road through the area, it is just a building in the way (Walter 2010a).

When the nature of reality is taken for granted, it is extremely difficult to come to grips with ontology. Returning to the example of Puerto Ricans in the U.S. Census, until the perceptions of Puerto Ricans themselves were solicited, it would have been extremely difficult for census takers to understand why there was any judgement involved in what they were doing—why they were not just counting the reality that was out there. And one's own understanding of reality can be very compelling, especially for dominant settler populations, where it is rarely challenged. It can feel just like common sense, and other ways of being and conceptualizing reality seem nonsensical. What these other ways of being and perceiving reality actually are is ontologically untranslatable. For Indigenous people and other "others," the ongoing clash between their own ontology and the governing societal understandings illuminates ontological boundaries.

The ontological framework of researchers and funders, then, plays a critical role in determining how research is perceived, conceptualized, and practiced. Researchers' ontologies mold how they think about the world. They are what set the boundaries—usually invisible—around what research is doable, and how. They shape researchers' understandings of what topics seem worthy and what questions can reasonably be asked. Ontology opens certain topics and questions, just as it forecloses others. Most fundamentally, researchers' ontological frameworks also influence perceptions of what humans *are*, their way of being. Observable examples of presumptive ways of being can be found within all disciplinary ontological frames. *Homo economicus*, so beloved by economists, is a prime example. As the theoretical base of classical economics and present day market economics, *homo economicus*, or "economic man," presumes that people are rational and self-interested actors who have the ability to make informed judgments. From this understanding of reality, people will always attempt to maximize utility for themselves as either producers or consumers. The broad strokes of such models miss, of course, the historical embeddedness of what those terms *mean* within any given culture. Altruism, especially anonymous or unacknowledged altruism, is ontologically untranslatable as a way of being for *homo economicus*.

History also provides examples of how conceptions of reality change observably at the societal level. For instance, before the European enlightenment, Europeans believed that the earth lay at the center of the solar system. This taken-for-granted reality was embedded in a specifically European ontology—the perception that humans *were* God's special creation, superior to other creatures over which God had given humans dominion. As Galileo found out (at great personal cost), counter suggestions were considered completely ludicrous, even dangerous or heretical. But wait, you might argue, those perceptions of reality were changed by the provision of hard scientific evidence to support an alternative perception. And this is so; the ontological base was exposed as a chimera and so was replaced by another. Yet, still now, the majority of individuals in our society equally accept these alternate views of reality without a scintilla of knowledge of how the universe or DNA works. Why? Because it is what we have been authoritatively told. Our view of reality in these areas, therefore, is still set the same way as those of the pre-Enlightment era, by social and cultural consensus rather than acontextual evidence—or at least, only a narrow band of evidence is deemed appropriate for answering research questions.

Perceptions of reality, therefore, were and remain held up by a framework of beliefs about "the way things are" and the way people and the social world understand and act on their social worlds. This is not to argue, of course, that there are no realities and that all things are relative. What it does mean, however, is that as human beings we all live in a world about which our frame of reference is socially constructed and hence cognitively constricted. More importantly, it is incredibly difficult to view that world outside of this frame of reference and, insofar as this is true, it serves to shape and contain our perceptions of reality. As embedded members of dominant society in colonized first world nations, researchers' reality of the research topic, object, or objective is framed by dominant perceptions of that world and the humans that inhabit it.

Theoretical Frame and Methods

Theoretical frameworks make up the next aspect of methodology. It is not within the purview of this book to analyze the broad range of theoretical frames, for several reasons. First, apart from macro theories that cross disciplinary boundaries (for example, Marxism), they tend to be located within a particular discipline. As such, a researcher's selection of a theoretical frame tends to be informed by the researcher's disciplinary training and the range limited only by the breadth of literature and other research deemed relevant to the field of study. However, we want to emphasize that like data, theory is not neutral. This claim of the lack of neutrality concerns more than the fact that theories are competing sets of ideas, or that many theoretical frames, at least those connected to the social world, are clearly ideologically aligned.

Our argument is more complex: in much Western colonizing settler framed research, the theoretical frame is positioned as the lens through which the research is approached, conducted, and interpreted. It is essentially positioned as the non-method bit of methodology. We do not dispute that a researcher's theoretical frame and his or her methodology are linked. What we question, rather, is the order. More specifically, we argue that the researcher's standpoint dictates how he or she makes sense of the many competing theoretical frames and therefore selects it (or them) as most appropriate for the research. Theoretical framework selection is thus an ontologically, axiologically, and epistemologically driven task. Sense-making, or the alignment of a particular theory with how we view our topic, is framed by the researcher's standpoint and the original theorist and the disciplinary field to which the researcher and the theory are situated.

Early feminist scholars researching topics such as the family, for example, found that the existing literature was predominantly built on theoretical frameworks that reflected the standpoint of earlier researchers, white middle class males. Talcott Parsons had theorized the family as reducible to two basic functions, the primary socialization of children and the stabilizations of adult personalities. Within these functions men and women had prescribed "natural" roles. Others, such as John Bowlby's theory of the psychological need of children to be cared for intensively by their mother, reinforced the idea of a natural division of household labor and relatively fixed gender roles (cited in van Krieken et al. 2000). Feminist researchers' response was to develop new theoretical frameworks that better reflected their own standpoint. Annie Oakley (1974), as per our earlier example of gendered knowledges, theorized that the household division of labor, rather than being natural, was about patriarchy and the power of men over women.

Additionally, while commonly presented as universal, the vast majority of existing and commonly used theoretical frames have similar social position origins. Most emerge from the Metropole (Connell 2007)—a white European and North American upper middle class, mostly male realm—and it shows. They are rarely presented this way, however, either by their creators or their users. Connell (2007) has argued that the gendered, raced, and geographical positions of theoretical frames tend to be acknowledged only if the theorist is not male, not white, not middle class, and/or not from a northern hemisphere, Western society. In this case this "difference" is frequently used to delimit the social spaces within which theory has relevance; that is, feminist theory is usually labelled as such and restricted to topics that focus on gender.

Yet the standpoints of all theorizers are reflected in the theories they produce. The groundbreaking work of Pierre Bourdieu on the mechanisms of social inequality is instructive in this context. Bourdieu, a white Frenchman, was born in the early part of the twentieth century and schooled initially in the discipline of philosophy. Although his family was lower middle class (his father was a peasant-turned-postal worker), he rose to occupy the Chair of Sociology at the College de France (Swartz 1997). His academic career, while eventually stellar, was not a linear rise to the top, however. Bourdieu's own social position, therefore, helps to explain his conceptual emphasis on the workings of social class. We might speculate that his lack of high status family background, common amongst his academic peers and rivals, stimulated insights into how class—and the social, cultural, and economic capitals bound to social classes—shapes how we see and experience the world, as well as shaping our life trajectories. His relegation of gender and race to second order dimensions of inequality are also likely influenced by his dominant gender and race position. In Bourdieu's experience, it seems, they were not as ontologically coherent as class. As such, while powerful, Bourdieu's work, as for us all, is both aided and limited by his own social positioning, and thus standpoint.

While the theoretical frames being formulated by Indigenous scholars are rapidly expanding beyond Western academic norms, the established theoretical frames available within disciplines are still largely those of white Western northern hemisphere sources. For Indigenous researchers this does not mean that such theories cannot be useful; they can. The insights and theoretical understandings of the Western canon can be, and are, reshaped to serve Indigenous needs. For example, Moreton-Robinson (2006) utilizes the work of Michel Foucault to extrapolate her theory of white possession. In particular, she makes use of his theoretical framework on rights, regimes of truth, and surveillance for analyzing how colonial possession (of Indigenous lands, peoples, cultures) is a mode of white rationality. This rationality defines and circumscribes Indigenous sovereignty. The discourse of rights in colonized first world nations, Moreton-Robinson argues, supports white possession through regulatory mechanisms including legal decisions, government legislation and policy.

Likewise, her discussion of Foucault's notion of discursive frameworks helps us understand how Indigenous peoples come to be understood as "known" rather than as "knowers" and, in particular, as knowers of whiteness (Moreton-Robinson 2004).

As Indigenous researchers we must be careful not to discard the value of the scholarship merely because Indigenous scholars did not develop it. This would be a serious, needless, and potentially disabling error. In Chapter 3 we explain in more depth the relationship between Indigeneity and modernity because we think it is critical not to get ourselves caught up in the "rule of difference" (Chatterjee 1993) that has shaped the last five centuries of global colonial projects. What it *does* mean, however, is that theoretical frames emanating from Indigenous and non-Indigenous disciplinary sources and knowledge production theoretical frames should be subject to the same critically rigorous examination about the standpoint "who" and the "what" they represent. What is it about these particular theoretical frames that does, or does not, make sense to us, and, perhaps more importantly, what is it about us that means we are in sync with this or these frameworks and not others.

Finally, as quantitative researchers, the methods we use (as distinct from our methodology) are statistical, mathematical, or computational techniques. The who, how, and what of how we use our method is, of course, definitively shaped by the researcher's standpoint. Who is asked what, in what manner, by whom, for what purpose, and how those responses are then analyzed, interpreted, and presented are, we argue, more a product of that standpoint than they are of the topic of the research. As argued in Chapter 1, Indigenous statistics in particular make the standpoint from which these data are created apparent. They emerge from the conduct of surveys, census or administrative data collections that have been designed, developed, analyzed, and reported from a particular, usually dominant, societal standpoint. For colonized first world Indigenous peoples this dominant societal standpoint is a reflection of its Western, white, colonizing settler society origins. We want to make clear that we are not questioning the validity of statistical analysis techniques such as ordinary least squares regression, factor analysis, chi square, correlation, or the myriad of other statistical tools. Rather, it is the powerful influence of the usually invisible standpoints that inform what data are gathered, by whom, and for what purpose that shapes how we use our quantitative methods.

Conclusion

Clearly, the approach we have outlined in this chapter will make some people uncomfortable, on both sides of the methodological rail. For those who have been trained in, and thus cling to, a notion of objective (as opposed to biased) research, we appear to be suggesting that no such thing exists. We humbly suggest that we are in fact saying the opposite: that objectivity remains powerfully tethered to one's axiological, epistemological, and ontological position. Moreover, we want to stress that this tethering of research standpoint and methodology is a central facet of Western colonizer settler quantitative methodologies. Yes, standpoint is central to Indigenous quantitative methodologies, but this is the case for *all* research. However, Indigenous methodologists and researchers cannot be so blithely (and conveniently) unaware of this social positioning as are colonizer settler researchers, since our work is often positioned as more political simply because it is different from the status quo. More critically, as argued in the previous chapter, the standpoint of their methodology silences and obscures how colonizer settler researchers' values, knowledge hierarchies, and ways of being impact quantitative research on Indigenous issues, communities, and peoples in ways no less powerful for their invisibility.

On the other side of the rail, some are wedded to the *differentness* of Indigenous methodology as its defining feature. We appear to be refuting dissimilarity by suggesting that the building blocks of a methodology are the same regardless of whether our research engages with Indigenous or settler populations. Are we not, therefore, removing the central methodological pillars of Indigenous peoples' relationship to our land, territory, and communities? We disagree and suggest, again, that we are doing the opposite. Creating building blocks of a methodology helps us account not only for differences from and similarities to dominant colonizer settler methodological paradigms but also *their* differences from and similarities to ours.

This two way perspective is central to how we position first world Indigenous quantitative methodologies. When we conceive of Indigenous methodologies only in terms of difference, we value them for their separateness and ultimately opposition to colonizer paradigms. This is constraining because we can only be what they are not, we can only be measured in the extent of our difference from the unmarked, standard Western paradigms. To make matters worse, colonial settler paradigms tend to cannibalize Indigenous spaces as their own. That is to say, as non-Indigenous researchers begin to decolonize their methodologies and methods and venture into Indigenous research spaces formerly marginalized, they may begin to see these methodologies and methods as "normal." In these cases, those spaces, formerly Indigenous, now seem less so because white scholars come to inhabit them, physically and intellectually, and as such, *claim* them. Presuming the essential differentness of Indigeneity limits the what, where, and how we can engage in critique as Indigenous scholars (see Andersen 2009: 110). Spaces—all spaces—are not acontextually Indigenous or not. Rather, they are embedded in competing claims to their authenticity. As we explain in the next chapter, Indigenous methodologies, situated within the full spectrum of our Indigenous subjectivities, are much more than this.

Chapter 3

The Paradigm of Indigenous Methodologies

In order to develop an Indigenous quantitative methodology, we must first synthesize the overarching principles of all Indigenous methodologies. While the literature on Indigenous research methodologies of any kind is slim, the field is a vigorous and active domain of knowledge production. The ground-breaking work of noted Māori scholar Linda Tuhiwai Smith (1999) introduced the concept of Indigenous methodologies as fundamentally *differing* from Western traditions and sharing, across Indigenous nations, key tenets and underpinning philosophies. This scholarship set the stage for the acknowledgment of Indigenous research methodologies as a unique and valid methodological approach. It underscored how, globally, Indigenous peoples apply their own lenses, perspectives, and understandings to the research process. Indigenous research methodologies are emerging and developing at a rapid pace.

As Porsanger (2004) postulates, Indigenous methodological frames recognize knowledge as grounded in Indigenous ways of being, knowing, and doing in everyday life. From an Indigenous methodological frame all aspects of the research process must be reframed and redefined. The range of research spaces where Indigenous methodologies are producing new scholarship evidence the breadth and divergence of the outcomes of this process. For example, Tuhiwai Smith's (1999) groundbreaking work on decolonizing methodologies not only challenged how Indigenous peoples have come to be known and defined through the research methodology of the West but also demonstrated how research developed within a Kaupapa Māori methodology reframes all aspects of the research process. Sharing knowledge is a long-term commitment she argues, and our communities and our peoples know that knowledge is power, but the challenge for Indigenous researchers is to demystify and decolonize (16). Building on Tuhiwai Smith's legacy, Cree scholar Wilson (2008: 58) used an Indigenous methodological frame to investigate the experience of being an Indigenous scholar within university systems. If Indigenous ways of knowing have to be narrowed through one particular lens, he asserts, then that lens would be relationality, and this concept permeates the scholarly writing of Indigenous scholars. Other scholars like Dine academic Gail Cannella (Cannella and Manuelito 2008) draw on feminist decolonizing discourse to develop modes of research practice that emphasize Native epistemologies and spiritualities, concepts grounded in the Dine way of life. From such Indigenized practices, it is argued, an anti-colonial social science might emerge.

In the field of education Russell Bishop (2008) brings a Māori worldview to his outline of educational practice by using Whanau (extended family) as the basis of research. Developed within a Kaupapa Māori frame, such research uses Māori metaphors and repositions researchers within Māori sense-making contexts, with a focus on the centrality of relations to others to Māori epistemologies. Bishop (2008) further develops a culturally responsive pedagogy of relations. He describes this pedagogy as:

> education where power is shared between self-determining individuals within non-dominating relations of interdependence, where culture counts, and where learning is interactive, dialogic , and spirals and participants are connected and committed to one another through the establishment of a common vision of what constitutes educational excellence. (445–446)

Using this framework to compare narrations of students' classroom experiences and meanings with stories from parents, teachers, and principals, Bishop demonstrates a disparity in understandings and the pejorative power of pathologizing.

Storytelling, or "yarning" as it is referred to in Australia, also figures strongly within explications of Indigenous qualitative methodologies and methods as a form of communication and as a bearer of traditional knowledges. For example, Dawn Bessarab (2010), a Bardi/Indjarbardi scholar, incorporates the Australian Aboriginal communicative tradition of yarning as an information gathering tool into a qualitative analysis to explore the growing up, in family gendered experiences, of her participants. In her book, *Indigenous Methodologies: Characteristics, Conversations and Contexts*, Cree scholar Kovach (2009) takes storytelling as the center of the transmission of Indigenous epistemologies, knowledges, and teachings. Her explication of an Indigenous based approach incorporates Indigenous conceptual and analytical frames and the significance of stories in the conduct of culturally valid Indigenous qualitative research practice. In a similar vein Sioux literary scholar Cook-Lynn (2008) argues that storytelling and incorporating tribal culture, knowledges, and historical perspectives assist in both defining what Indigeneity is and clarifying the function of Indigenous origins in modern thought. Not only the stories coming through to Native American people from the past, but also the Indian stories being told today, she argues, are bearers of traditional Indian knowledge, history, and myth.

Notwithstanding the diversity of disciplines in which they have been developed and uses to which they have been put, Indigenous methodologies share some common philosophical premises that accord with some, if not all, of the facets outlined in Figure 2.1—our definition of a methodology. For example, Tuhiwai Smith (1999: 185) cites G. Smith's 1990 summary of Kaupapa Māori research as: related to "being Māori; is connected to Māori philosophy and principles; takes for granted the validity and legitimacy of Māori; the importance of Māori language and culture; and is concerned with the struggle for autonomy over Māori's own cultural well being." Similarly, Wilson (2008) argues that Indigenous research is the ceremony of maintaining accountability to *relationships*. For Indigenous peoples, he states, relationships don't just *shape* reality, they *are* reality. As such, Indigenous researchers must be accountable to all our relations in the way that we approach, perceive, and do research. Indigenous research, he contends, is the ceremony of maintaining accountability to these relationships. Martin Nakata (1998) challenged the Western knowledge systems' way of knowing Torres Strait Islander people by developing his own Torres Strait Islander standpoint. Meyer (2008) more specifically developed thematics for organizing the vast and seemingly limitless province of Indigenous knowledges according to her native Hawaiian epistemology by the use of body, mind, and spirit to triangulate the Hawaiian way of meaning. At the center of Meyer's framework is her positioning of "*all* ideas, *all* histories, *all* facts, and *all* theories" as interpretations (230, italics in original). This starting point, she argues, is essential to the conceptualization and operationalization of all methodologies.

Nurungga scholar Rigney (1997) and Nunukul/Bidjara scholar Martin (2003) each articulates a set of inter-related principles that informs his or her conceptualization of Indigenous methodology. In articulating Indigenist research, Rigney emphasizes political integrity, resistance as the emancipatory imperative, and the privileging of Indigenous voices, arguing that using such an approach means pushing boundaries "in order to make intellectual space for Indigenous cultural knowledge systems that were denied in the past" (2001: 9). In a broadly similar (though distinct) approach, Martin summarizes the shared philosophical underpinnings of Indigenous methodological framework into four theoretical principles: recognition of our worldviews, our knowledges, and our realities as distinctive and vital to our existence and survival while serving as a research framework; honoring Aboriginal social mores as essential processes through which we live, learn, and situate ourselves as Aboriginal people in our own lands and when in the lands of other Aboriginal peoples; emphasizing the social, historical, and political contexts which shape our experience, lives, positions, and futures; and privileging the voices, experiences, and lives of Aboriginal people and Aboriginal lands.

Grande (2008), like many other Indigenous scholars, describes the tensions of identity and the practice of research, a tension she negotiated via the conscious development of her own Native American Indigenous methodology, "Red Pedagogy." Red Pedagogy, Grande states, operates at the crossroads of Western critical pedagogy and Indigenous knowledge and is a space of engagement rather than a method or technique. Within this space it critically analyses the precepts of critical pedagogy on the basis of its Western roots, pinpointing where its assumptions diverge from critical Indigenous methodologies. In particular, Grande questions the capacity of any non-Indigenous pedagogies to truly theorize Indigenous identity, the notion of Indigenous sovereignty, and the sacredness of lands within an non-anthropocentric view of peoples, land, and natural resources (238). In her case study of culturally responsive pedagogy, Kau Kahakalau's (2004) Indigenous heuristic action research methodology integrates Hawaiian cultural protocols and Indigenous epistemology. This methodology frames Kakakalau's education research and includes as a central premise, the participation of the researcher within the research itself. As Kahakalua (2004: 22) states:

> As a native Hawaiian I bring to every task my *mana*, my personal power, which includes all my strengths; physical, emotional, intellectual, and spiritual. I also bring my personal skills and experiences, my hopes, my dreams, my visions, and my ancestral endowments, including the wisdom that my ancestors share with me while I sleep, as well as the knowledge my many teachers have imparted to me.

For Kahakalua (2004: 24) the development of her methodology shifted the research problematic from the students to the model of education. Her original research question changed from "How do we teach Hawaiian students to be *pono*?" to "What constitutes a quality K–12 model of education?" The results of Kahakalua's complex, rigorous, multi-method (qualitative and quantitative) research changed the way the education system is understood in Hawaii.

Indigenous methodologies inevitably also include an Indigenous perspective on research ethics. Using her own experience as a member of a working party to develop research processes involving Mi'kmaw knowledges, Canadian Indigenous scholar Battiste (2008) raised the clash of ethical values that continue to arise between Western researchers and Indigenous peoples in relation to Indigenous knowledges. Battiste contends that Indigenous knowledges are, and continue to be, culturally misappropriated by Western researchers. Noting that "few academic contexts exist within which to talk about Indigenous knowledge and heritage in an unprejudiced way" (503), Battiste critiques the value and validity of the standard academic ethical safeguards, such as including an Indigenous person on ethics committees. Such measures, she argues, never truly address the central issue of the ownership of the research and its outputs. She further contends that such individualizing practices fail to consider protection issues for the collective and as such may themselves contribute to the continued appropriation and pillaging of Indigenous culture, heritage, and knowledge.

Differentiating First World Indigenous Methodologies

Commonalities among the Indigenous methodologies do exist in some of the work of Indigenous scholars from outside the colonized first world. Building on the innovative work of Indigenous Mexican scholar Anzaldua (1987), Central American scholar Saavedra, for example, outlines with co-author Nymark a feminist borderland-mestizaje methodology (Saavedra and Nymark 2008). This methodology takes as its focus the analysis of the blank spots in dominant ideology and discourse in any analysis of gender, class, and race, especially as they relate to Chicana and Latina women. As such, borderland-mestizaje feminism emerges from the lived experiences of the (Indigenous) self and others and is perceived by Saavedra and Nymark as operating in the space between methodologies. Its fundamental role is to create the space for subversive ideas and practices with an end goal of transformation. Others, such as African scholar Chilisa (2012), premise their Indigenous methodological frame on understanding how non-academic knowledge systems fit within research paradigms. Utilizing a post-colonial frame, her focus is on paradigms and practices that highlight methodologies that support Indigenous epistemologies and honor integrative knowledge systems.

Methodological commonalities between first, second, and third world Indigenous scholars, however, do not necessarily result in globally applicable Indigenous methodologies. As explained in the Introduction, we do share a central critique of the dominance of the Western ontological base in the research interrogation of the Indigenous other. But the diversity of our histories, our contemporary and historical experiences of colonization, our traditional and contemporary cultural lives, and our current social, political, and economic positioning mean that often we are more different than we are similar. As such, our methodological frames will also be widely diverse.

Certainly, Indigenous scholars from around the world can and do learn from each other, as well as support each other in our quest to reshape research relating to our peoples. But we recognize that not only are there Indigenous methodologies rather than an Indigenous methodology, but that there are different categories of Indigenous methodologies. These should not be conflated, but rather recognized for the strengths each brings and the specificity of the contexts in which they apply. Categorizing Indigenous methodologies as a homogenous group risks essentializing Indigenous peoples even more than we do now. More critically, we cannot, and do not have the right to, speak to how Indigenous statistics and Indigenous quantitative methodologies are, or might be, practiced in other Indigenous peoples' countries that do not have similar colonizing antecedents as those in first world nations.

From our perspective, then, it is the centrality of the shared colonized histories and contemporary social, economic, and political positioning of Indigenous peoples living in Western colonized first world nations that bind our definition of Indigenous methodologies. Again, this is not to suggest that first world colonized peoples are the same, or that Indigenous methodologies developed within this context will equate to a prescriptive orthodoxy. We are not, and they do not. The conceptualization, operationalization, and most critically, research practice of the epistemologies, axiologies, and ontologies that underpin our methodologies occur in myriad ways and vary by researcher and by country and cultural belonging. Instead, we point to the similarities of our Anglo histo-colonizing antecedents, the consequent similarity of the institutions and instruments of the state that shape our contemporary colonizer settler interactions, our shared social and politically marginalized positioning within the (predominately) English speaking first world nations, and our mutual minority status as a platform and a strength in the development of an observably aligned paradigm of Indigenous quantitative methodologies.

These similarities inform the plethora of literature across disciplines that comparatively examine Indigenous issues across first world colonized nations. In the area of Indigenous rights, Ivison, Patton, and Sanders's (2000) edited collection relates to Indigenous peoples in Australia, Aotearoa New Zealand, and North America, and Havemann (1999) compares Australia, Canada, and New Zealand. Cottrell (2010) discusses the striking parallels of education experiences of Indigenous peoples in Canada, the United States, Australia, and New Zealand, and Cassidy (2006) compares the similarity of the removal and detaining of Aboriginal children in the twentieth century in Canada and Australia. On the colonizing process itself, Miller, Ruru, Behrendt, and Londberg (2010) explore how the doctrine of discovery was used to rationalize the colonization of the United States, Canada, Aotearoa New Zealand, and Australia. Comparative research, however, is not just about identifying the similarities of our historical and contemporary positioning. As Hayward (2010: 139) remarks in her comparison of Indigenous representation in Canada and New Zealand, "Comparative research is an empowering component of 'research as resistance' for scholars in Indigenous studies."

Our historical and contemporary similarities are also recognized by our respective nation-states. For example, the statistical entities of the state in first world colonizing nations tend to compare the "progress" of their own Indigenous populations across health, education, and socio-economic dimensions with those of other first world colonizing states. In Australia, the Australian Institute of Health and Welfare (AIHW 2011b), for example, compares the life expectancy of Aboriginal and Torres Strait Islander peoples with Indigenous people in New Zealand, Canada, and the United States. Though less so, Canada has undertaken comparisons between Indigenous peoples in Canada and elsewhere using the United Nations' Human Development Index (see, for example, Cooke et al. 2007).

Developing the Paradigm of Indigenous Quantitative Methodologies

Indigenous methodologies share underpinning philosophical principles but still vary in their focus, topic, approach, and utility of method. That said, a body of work in Indigenous quantitative methodology does not, as yet, exist to any substantive degree. Thus far, the field of Indigenous methodologies has been dominated by debates around Indigenous *qualitative* methodologies. Indeed, qualitative research techniques have generally been seen by Indigenous researchers to fit more squarely with Indigenous agendas and community interests than quantitative methods, despite the power and reach of the latter. As a result, their use is comparatively rare among Indigenous researchers. Epidemiology is probably one of the few quantitative fields to have an observable Indigenous presence, with Māori scholars especially prominent in their field. For example, Simmonds, Robson, Cram, and Purdie (2008) write on Kaupapa Māori epidemiology, and the Te Rōpū Rangahau Hauroa A Eru Pōmare Centre at the Wellington School of Medicine conspicuously places its research within a Kaupapa Māori space. Others, such as Māori demographer Tahu Kukutai (2011; 2012), also stand out. However, the need for more Indigenous quantitative researchers and a body of work on Indigenous quantitative methodologies to inform their practice is vital if Indigenous peoples are to take hold of the reins of knowledge production about ourselves and our social relations.

A principle premise of this book, to paraphrase Bourdieu (1991), is that research methodologies are always open to excluded groups to develop heretical discourses and categories and practices that go against the official grain. Discourses by their nature evolve and change as power relations evolve and change, and those from excluded groups, by the insights derived from their positionality within those discourses, are uniquely positioned to challenge the status quo. Developing heretical discourses on how Indigenous statistics are created, disseminated, and interpreted is the job of quantitative Indigenous researchers. Our first imperative is to decouple and segregate, intellectually as well as practically, the research method (statistics) from its standard methodological framing. This decoupling is necessary to create some space between the narrowly conceived aspects of Indigeneity traditionally associated with Indigenous quantitative research that in turn have created a "deficit-based" visage of Indigeneity and the use of statistical analytical techniques themselves (see Chapter 1). Our argument is that methodology, rather than the method of analysis, contains the cultural, social, and consequently, political meanings of research process and practice. And it is within Western settler quantitative methodological frames that the continuing authorization of our Indigenous peoples as the "other"' occurs.

Indigenous Statistical Space

In claiming statistical space is Indigenous, we are mindful that Indigenous quantitative research involves more than an Indigenous researcher leading research on Indigenous related topics. Despite this caution, we also need to acknowledge that the repositioning of the Indigene within the research process and practice is the starting point of an Indigenous quantitative methodological frame. Moving the Indigene from research object to director—from "known" to "knower"—can, in itself, be methodologically transformative. Indigenous researchers placing themselves (rather than being placed) at the forefront immediately alters the research practice terrain. But we suggest that in itself, this is not enough.

The terrain of Indigenous quantitative methodology is currently largely uncharted. It is necessary to explore, identify, and establish parameters to our conceptualization and operationalization of Indigenous quantitative methodologies. We now detail four such parameters. These are overlapping in practice but divided here to demonstrate their separate influences on Indigenous quantitative methodologies. To establish these parameters we must delineate:

1. the "fit" of the quantitative within Indigenous methodologies;
2. modernity and Indigenous quantitative methodologies;
3. our position within the field of quantitative methodologies; and
4. the purview of Indigenous quantitative methodologies.

The Fit of the Quantitative within Indigenous Methodologies

Though to many it is heretical to say so, there is nothing necessarily "less Indigenous" about quantitative than qualitative methodologies. While the field of Indigenous methodologies has been dominated by qualitative approaches, quantitative methods fit equally well within an Indigenous methodological frame and can speak to elements of our Indigeneity. The current tendency within Indigenous methodologies to concentrate on qualitative practice has left a large and troubling gap. As we argue further in Chapter 6, Indigenous scholars are currently limited in what we teach our students about Indigeneity *and* the kinds of official representations of Indigeneity that get produced because there are not enough of us involved in the "statistical cycle" (described in Chapter 1)—the on-going process of envisioning, commissioning, collecting, analysing, and interpreting statistics to engender a more robust conversation. This has serious and unfortunate consequences for the production of knowledge about Indigenous sociality, particularly in the numerous official contexts within which they are used.

As quantitative Indigenous scholars, we are sensitive to the near absence of discussion of the quantitative within the field of Indigenous methodologies. This gap is reinforced by the propensity of qualitative Indigenous methodologists to legitimize the authenticity of their approaches by contrasting their Indigenous epistemological base with an inferred epistemologically constricted premise of quantitative methods, especially in relation to the now outmoded idea of equating Western quantitative methodologies with positivism. Indigenous qualitative researchers are not alone in this practice. Western qualitative researchers have long set up their own qualitative framework in opposition to quantitative techniques, despite the false dichotomizing it requires. For example, on page one of their book on in-depth interviewing, Minichiello, Aroni, Timewell, and Alexander (1990) write that most research books are written from a quantitative research frame, which they define as "methods based on positivist understanding of social reality." Qualitative research, they add, is in opposition to this way of seeing the world (1990:2). What is unique about how quantitative methodology is positioned within current writing on Indigenous methodologies is that they are by their way of doing research, *ipso facto*, unsuitable for the study of Indigeneity (see Gilchrist 1997).

We argue that such arguments, although probably benign in intent, are not helpful to building more sophisticated relationships between Indigeneity and quantitative knowledge. No convincing arguments or evidence is given to support the inferred claims that some methods are suited for adaptation into Indigenous methodologies, while others are doomed by their institutional genealogies. Moreover, it should be clear by now that the absence of quantitative methods from the research armory of Indigenous scholars is problematic. Restrictions on how we engage in research as *Indigenous* scholars disarms us in the very terrain where we need to be most active, the relations of power that allow current statistical analysis *of us* to be accepted as exhaustive descriptions and definitions of who we are.

An example from African American scholarship elucidates our argument. Robin Kelley (1997: 17) suggested that during the 1970s (white American) social scientists had reduced blackness to ghetto culture in much the same way as they do so now with respect to Indigenous communities. As Kelley (1997:

16) put it, "Sociologists, anthropologists, political scientists and economists compete for huge grants…to measure everything measurable in order to get a handle on the newest internal threat to civilization." Statistical constructions were ordered according to more or less tacit social disorganization theses that perceived black "ghetto" culture either as a manifestation of individual pathologies (drugs or sexualized behavior) or as a reaction to and means of enduring poverty and racism.[1]

In response, Kelley (1997: 9–10) articulated a concept of black *density*. Density speaks to numerous subject positions that eclipse standard tropes about African American blackness to come to terms with a more complex "immediacy" which defies easy (academic) description. Much official statistical analysis about Indigenous communities is similarly obsessed with narrow aspects of our daily life, as explored in previous chapters, particularly around the apparent "truth" of our social disadvantage, as though those conditions—and resistance to them—constitute all there is to know about us, or the only way we *can* be known in quantitative contexts. As articulated by Kelley, the theorization of such a narrow band of research questions led to authoritative, and thus frequently unchallenged, definitions of who we are and the essence of our social relations.

Certainly, dangers exist in qualifying Indigenous colonial experiences in terms of larger forms of oppression impacting other racialized entities. Not the least of these is the erasure of an important difference between Indigenous and other disadvantaged groups: our sovereignty. Nonetheless, whitestream representations of blackness operate according to similar epistemological and ontological forms of abstraction. Like blackness, Indigeneity is often (still) positioned in opposition to white/colonial identity along a series of binary oppositions that labor to reaffirm their supposed superiority and our apparent primitiveness. And like blackness, Indigenous complexity has been reduced in time and space through apparently objective, logical markers that come to stand in for our sociality itself —that is, the lens through which officials "look" at our communities comes to stand in for the communities themselves.

Indeed, our respective nation-states and social researchers are keen to fix us in time (that is, the past) and space. Our growing urban presence has largely been ignored within the research and public discourse against a heavy concentration of those peoples among us living remotely in more rural settings (see Peters and Andersen 2013). For example, as far back as 1981, Aboriginal scholar Marcia Langton railed against the lack of research by Australian social scientists into urban Aboriginal life and the lack of acknowledgment that Aboriginal culture could and did exist within urban settings (Langton 1981: 16), despite the fact that four in five Indigenous people live in urban areas. In Canada, despite the fact that roughly half of all Aboriginal peoples live in urban areas, only a single chapter in the massive 1996 *Royal Commission on Aboriginal Peoples* was dedicated to urban issues. As we detail more in the next two chapters, Indigenous quantitative methodologies not only challenge the legitimacy of these discourses, they provide the evidentiary base for new and efficacious competing discourses.

The placement of artificial and unnecessarily restrictive boundaries around the conceptualization of *bona fide* Indigenous methodologies works against Indigenous interests. And while allusions to the continued power of our traditional Indigenous ontologies and epistemologies within methodological descriptions operate as arenas of resistance to colonial projects, they also (unnecessarily) limit the range of our conceptual toolbox for dealing with contemporary issues. "Tradition" still holds epistemic and ontological salience, but as we argue in the next section, its *automatic* precedence is essentializing and epistemologically and ontologically restrictive. It also is indicative of the numerous ways in which the cultural power of first world nation-states does not merely oppress, but seduces as well.[2] The logical endpoint of these anchoring conceptions denies Indigenous methodologies the central role they *ought* to play in denaturalizing dominant constructions of Indigeneity, a task which must make use of *all* available theories and methods, *especially* quantitative knowledge. As we explain next, the marginalization of quantitative methods as Indigenous ignores those methodologies most able to deal with powerful actors such as actors of nation-state agencies.

Modernity and Indigenous Quantitative Methodologies

We also assert that the binary between "modernity" and "tradition" is a false one. This is a bold claim and in the spirit of inviting what we see as a sorely needed discussion on the relationship of that binary to an equally popular one—quantitative/qualitative—we should probably explain to readers what we mean when we use the term 'modernity' and why we think that Indigenous methodologies and modernity do not require the split between quantitative and qualitative (and the marginalization of the former) that the field appears to have created.

We use the term 'modernity' to signify the here and now in our respective colonizing settler nation-states. The full complexity of the concept of modernity is far beyond our ability to define it here, except to say that we generally position it to refer to the political, economic, social, and culture changes produced in the development of the modern state, the capitalist economy, and the industrial revolution (see Hall 1995). In this context, we are interested in those aspects of modernity that speak to: 1) the rise in secular forms of political power and authority, with allied notions of sovereignty and legitimacy; 2) exchange economies, the stabilized consumption of market commodities, and the accumulation of wealth and private property; 3) the replacement of traditional hierarchies of order with new divisions of labor (including patriarchal); 4) the rise of secular culture and the associated decline of religious worldviews; 5) the novel ways through which knowledge was produced and classified; and finally, 6) the growth of nationalism (see Hall 1995: 8–9).

Of course, broad definitions like this, while orienting, are not as helpful to exploring more specific concerns like those discussed here. Hence, the particular "node" of modernity we make use of in this book refers more specifically to changes in the post-WWII period in those countries like Australia, Canada, Aotearoa New Zealand, and the United States, in which strategies for governing Indigenous peoples underwent fairly profound changes from "assimilationist" to "integrative" modes that fit more squarely with their own self-conceptions of liberalism. In this context, we do not see a useful distinction between modernity and colonization since, in the context of the nation-states we discuss, they amounted to the same thing in practice. Nonetheless, while we agree that within these societies, our traditional knowledges remain vitally important and continuing aspects of who and how we are as Indigenous peoples, we must nonetheless make use of *all* of our Indigenous knowledges, not just those created in the eras preceding modernity and our interactions with an investment in it.

Conceptions of Indigenous knowledge that fail to account for *and make use of* this newer complexity epistemologically bind our research to specific cultural and traditional spaces. We cannot afford to be so bound. Indigenous methodologies are much more than methodologies built on culture and/or traditional and/or local knowledges relegated to some (more or less) mythologized past. For example, in their justifiably lauded 2008 *Handbook of Critical and Indigenous Methodologies,* Denzin, Lincoln, and Tuhiwai Smith define Indigenous methodologies as "research by and for indigenous peoples, using traditions and methods drawn from the traditions and knowledges of those peoples" (cited in Denzin, Lincoln, and Tuhiwai Smith, from Evans, Hole, Berg, Hutchinson, and Sookraj forthcoming). While nothing in this definition *necessarily* excludes quantitative methods, the ways that "traditions" and "knowledges" are usually defined devalue quantitative methodologies as a central form of modern knowledge production that is, therefore, dismissed as an important ally to Indigenous cultural and political projects.

The prominence of the Denizen et al. text and its definition compels us, in this section, to engage in a deeper discussion about the relationship between Indigeneity and contemporary everyday life in our first world nations and, more precisely, the role of quantitative knowledge in this context. And incidentally, this realization does not come from any particular critiques of Indigenous methodologists themselves; rather, it speaks to the wholesale marginalization of quantitative methods from that field of inquiry—simply put, no one writes about it.

Our broader point—and one which we think most Indigenous methodolo-gists would agree with—is this: despite the deliberate efforts of colonial projects, within each of our first world nation-states our communities and peoples are still here as complex, dynamic, and growing communities. The curved wall of the National Museum of the American Indian in Washington proclaims that "WE ARE THE EVIDENCE." This evidence reflects not just the concerted endeavors to destroy and/or assimilate us but evidence of our continued existence and the ongoing vibrancy and vigor of our communities, societies, and peoples. We are part of our respective modern societies, not a remnant of the past, and Indigenous methodologies that fail to engage in a primary language of modern power—quantitative methods—miss out on a crucial tool, not only for resisting colonial projects but, more fundamentally, for constituting the social representations through which Indigeneity is understood by the public at large. Sahlins (1999) summed up the power of the "tradition/modernity" binary by positing that the relationship between Indigeneity and modernity skewers the pretentions of early-to-mid twentieth century anthropological thinking poised to document the logical endpoint of effects of modernity on Indigenous peoples: our extinction. In this context, his phrase evokes the extent to which Indigenous collectivities have retained the principles that animate our social relations, not just *in spite of,* but in some cases *because of,* its social processes. Indeed, for many of our peoples, our supposedly "traditional" cultures had already been changed by decades or even centuries of interaction with capitalism/colonialism by the time anthropolo-gists began to remark on our cultural difference. More pertinently, our traditional forms of existence were/are not necessarily incommensurable with the evolving cultures and practices of capitalism/colonialism (Salhins 1999).

Modernity is thus not patently coterminous with the destruction of Indigenous societies, communities, cultures, and ways of being, knowing, see-ing, and acting: we are still here. To be crystal clear, however, this observation is not to suggest that modernity—the growth of the modern state, colonialism, and so forth—is not as bad as it has been made out to be. Rather, our point is that it was and is never as *effective* as its engineers' pretensions and hubris made and make it out to be. We resisted and incorporated as required to survive its storms, and these strategies constitutively impacted our sense of Indigeneity. However, modernity/colonialism was never as powerful or as far-reaching as its progenitors presented it, nor were its various forms of power as unidirectional.

Few scholars who undertake Indigenous community research would quarrel with the argument that our communities differ in fundamental ways from dominant, whitestream society. We agree. Yet these same scholars must also acknowledge that our communities and nations are embedded within their respective first world nation-states in complex and longstanding ways. Regardless of where or how we live, we can no longer, and have not been able to for a very long time, exist outside our colonizing nation-states, though our degrees of engagement vary in kind and degree. Nonetheless, we live our daily lives awash in a sea of quantitative methodologies through which modern nation-states govern. Telephone numbers, credit cards, employee numbers, tax forms, health information—in these and enumerable other contexts, we continue to recognize our many selves in the categories expressed through these numbers. If we live in modernity and if we "continue to exist" as Indigenous peoples, there is absolutely no reason to think that how we learn to live in and navigate these social relations cannot or should not be thought of as valuable Indigenous knowledge.

Our embeddedness and our investments thus play a powerful part in shaping our contemporary Indigeneity—we speak the official languages of the state (almost always not our own); we engage in various forms of technology to facilitate ceremony (whether driving out to ceremonial sites or phoning or even Facebooking to set up meeting times); we eat food and drink liquids that are not only not traditional but in fact have proven immensely harmful to us. However, none of these social factors necessarily makes us "less" Indigenous, since these trappings of modernity were also faced, in their contemporaneous forms, by our ancestors. Nonetheless, the failure to heed this social fact pushes us unnecessarily and uncomfortably close to an "Aboriginalist discourse" (Attwood 1992) that defines us by who, apparently, we are not: white/capitalist/ secular/*modern*. Indigenous scholars and our allies have labored too intensively to interrogate and denaturalize such reductive logics to allow these constrictions to regain traction.[3]

Further, the reduction of Indigenous methodologies, quantitative or qualitative, to tradition and culture rearticulates a standard trope for positioning Indigenous authenticity that is heavily invested in by our colonizing settler powerbrokers. For example, Canadian Aboriginal rights law is ordered precisely according to juridical notions about what apparently makes Indigenous communities *truly* Indigenous, namely, our pre-contact occupation. Similarly, in Australia, under the Native Title Act 1993, groups must be able to demonstrate both that they are descended from the Aboriginal group who occupied the land at the time of the British claiming of the continent (1788) and that over the ensuing generations they have maintained an unbroken traditional connection to that land. The lived result is that the many peoples forcibly removed from country and cultural practices forbidden in constraining Aboriginal missions are deemed to have their claims to country legally extinguished. Moreover, it is only pre 1788 culture that is recognized. Cultural reinvigoration, such as that argued by the Yorta Yorta people, the traditional owners of the country on which the city of Melbourne now sits, is not valid. Their application was rejected on the basis that they had lost their connection with the traditional law and custom that would have sustained native title (Keen 1999).

This should not surprise us. Whitestream colonizing societies are at their most magnanimous when recognizing symbols of difference, since, according to Claude Denis (1997: 83), these societies have always "relied on a rhetoric of cultural difference to ensure the rule of the whitestream over non-European peoples." Yet our contemporary Indigenous communities constitute complex, tangled mélanges of difference and sameness, exoticism and familiarity. Thus, our critique is one familiar to post-structuralist/post-colonialist debates about authenticity, namely, that "the rhetoric of difference is a double-edged sword: a claim to difference can lead to (a degree of) empowerment at the same time that it creates and sustains images of the radical other, who is always subordinate" (Denis 1997: 83).

In sum, an emphasis on Indigenous tradition within our research methodologies vastly oversimplifies the complex set of relations within and through which Indigenous collectivities and subjectivities contemporarily manifest themselves. This simplism marginalizes the complex ways in which our Indigenous habitus (to borrow from Bourdieu 1984) is inevitably and irrevocably constituted in and by the fields of power we cohabit. And for good and ill, these fields of power are inextricably located within relations of modernity. So while we do not contest the centering of Indigenous communities and nations at the forefront of research within an Indigenous methodology, analysis without regard to the complex societal positioning of those communities and nations is problematic.

More specifically, our point is that in the attempt to analytically separate Indigenous communities from the broader social fabric of dominant, whitestream society, we have effectively removed a large part of our arsenal for combating the damaging (not to mention plainly inaccurate!) representations of Indigeneity woven into larger society. As we argue, one of the impacts of this kind of thinking has been the creation and encrustation of "deficit-model" based policy understandings of Indigeneity that dominate quantitative analyses of Indigeneity. To repeat: our point is not that models that emphasize our disadvantage are wrong. Rather, our point is that they are neither exhaustive nor contextual, nor do they produce the only legitimate statistics depictions of Indigenous communities.

This discussion brings us back to definitions and understandings of Indigenous methodologies. Indigenous knowledges are a central component of Indigenous quantitative methodologies, but such knowledges are not (and should not be) restricted to historical knowledges. Indigenous societies *evolve*, and the knowledges we bring to the research process and its methodological base must reflect the evolutions of our ontologies, axiologies, and epistemologies. Thus, quantitative methodologies can reflect Indigenous standpoints, but they do so within a broader understanding of our investment in modernity and modern nation-states. These can and do encompass and are related to all areas of the modern societal existence of first world Indigenous peoples. That they should do so is only logical. Modernity in all its aspects is the primary shaper of the life circumstances of Indigenous peoples in colonized first world nation-states, both in terms of our investment in and our resistance to it.

Position within the Field of Quantitative Methodologies

Indigenous quantitative methodologies are distinct from, but not necessarily dichotomous with, Western-based quantitative methodologies. Yet, a layered understanding of who we are and how we are Indigenous researchers (such as, for example, that articulated by Salhins [1999]) is not a dominant one. Instead, much of the current theoretical discussion on methodologies presupposes that to be authentically Indigenous is to be situated in tension with colonizer settler research paradigms. This, we argue, is (or can be) a serious misapprehension. While the dissimilarity of the standpoints will necessarily result in divergence between Western and Indigenous quantitative methodologies, this difference should not be conflated with the reverse: to differ from Western quantitative methodology is not the same as opposing it. Nor, as is the practice in much of the current discussion of Indigenous methodologies, should difference from colonizer settler methodologies sit at the core of what makes Indigenous methodology Indigenous.

In addition to eliding the boundaries of the development-based thinking currently dominating quantitative configurations of Aboriginal communities, we are not claiming that being Indigenous gives us answers that others could not find (although it might). Rather, we suggest that it increases the likelihood that we will ask *questions* that others have not and fashion categories that heretofore have not been used. Indigenous *quantitative* methods lay down an explicit challenge to the current boundaries of what counts as Indigenous knowledge. Certainly, statistical techniques cannot measure all or even most aspects of Indigenous sociality. But neither can Indigenous traditional knowledge-based research methods and methodologies—for example, how would Indigenous methodologists assist an Indigenous community who wanted to create a questionnaire to gauge Internet use in their community or wanted to compare water quality samples to those taken by state actors?

Properly conceived and executed quantitative evidence simply "speaks back to the state" in a manner that both incorporates Indigenous knowledges and is ontologically translatable to state actors. As such, an Aboriginal investment in the statistical form of our identities should be included in *any* discussion of Indigenous knowledge. We do not seek to replace more qualitatively oriented knowledge but, rather, to demonstrate that the deployment of qualitative or quantitative methodologies is equally appropriate depending on the research problematic. Both can be equally authentically operationalized within an Indigenous methodology.

As such, we critique what we see as an unnecessarily narrow and inflexible construction of Indigenous subjectivity within methodology. Such approaches can be construed as buying in to the identity discourse that argues that one's authenticity as an Indigenous person can only be evaluated in terms of one's difference from "whiteness"—speaking language, possessing an Indigenous "look," growing up in an Indigenous community, and so on. We do not, of course, reject the distinctiveness of Indigenous methodologies or, for that matter, Indigenous peoples. But we do reject the idea that Indigenous individuals and communities *have* to be different, and the alignment of such differentness to their white settler majority population definitions of Indigeneity. This is problematic not least because, as described in Chapter 2, as white researchers begin to decolonize and reach into Indigenous spaces, what happens when they attempt to claim those analytical spaces as their own? Are spaces long understood as Indigenous spaces now less so simply because state or university researchers (for example) also claim them?

Of course Indigenous methodologies hold Indigenous values and viewpoints at their center, but positioning these viewpoints only in terms of their apparent difference marginalizes our position as knowers of whiteness as well. A full consideration of the power and utility of quantitatively produced Indigenous knowledge requires that we "crack open" Indigeneity to denaturalize what we see as the ontologies of our respective colonizer settlers' whiteness. It is these particular practices of whiteness that reproduce and legitimate representations of Indigeneity that are tied only to discourses and practices of our difference. To conceive of our Indigeneity in these terms is to legitimize that discourse. Rather, we make an alternative argument that an appreciation of our full density/complexity/modernity must account for what Hokowhitu (2009) terms "Indigeneity of immediacy" as outlined in Chapter 1.

As scholars is it easy to see the seductive nature of simplistic notions of Indigeneity-as-difference. Indeed, across our nation-states, "state of the discipline" pieces in Indigenous Studies often begin by discussing the disciplinary content and boundaries thought to distinguish our scholarship from that of longer standing disciplines (see, for example, Cook-Lynn 1998; Weaver 2007). In a U.S. context, for example, Native American scholar Clara Sue Kidwell (2009: 6) suggests that such discussions play out in a tension between two poles of analysis: *essentialism/difference* and *adaptation/assimilation*. The essentialism cluster is rooted in an extreme form of post-colonialism (her term) which "implies that [Indigenous] ways of thinking existed before colonialism and remain unknowable by anyone outside those cultures. [Indigenous Studies] can recover the long-suppressed values, epistemologies, and voices from colonial oppression"

(Kidwell 2009: 6). Conversely, adaptation clusters typically emphasize the agency of Indigenous collectivities in the face of whitestream colonialism, the ways in which Indigenous peoples both colluded with and resisted (in her case) U.S. policies. As with the essentialism cluster, Kidwell (2009: 6) argues that in its extreme variant, "the idea of adaptation, or acculturation, or agency represents the ultimate disappearance of a distinctive [Indigenous] identity into [modernity] as citizens of the colonial nation states in which they live."

We agree that colonizer settler quantitative methodological orientations are beset with problematic concepts and practices in their engagement with things Indigenous. However, we argue that supposing a binary between Indigeneity and the immediacy of everyday Indigenous life (Hokowhitu 2009) is both false and misleading. As Hokowhitu argues, the tendency of many Indigenous and non-Indigenous scholars to focus on tradition and culture has encouraged the idea that cultural knowledge is beyond their lived experience. Using the example of Māori culture, he argues that such discussions seldom refer to everyday practices, such as the importance of the sport of rugby for contemporary cultures of Māori masculinity. Positioning Indigenous methodologies, therefore, as somehow removed from everyday Indigenous life and as the converse of colonizer settler disciplinary research, limits and constrains our methodological and research range of topics regarding what makes Indigenous peoples *truly* Indigenous and what colonizer settler methodologies remain unable to explain.

Such constraints leave little analytical purchase to deal with the complexities of being Indigenous in modern, Western societies, with respect to how we identify ourselves, how we critique dominant, whitestream representations, or how we employ colonizer settler discursive authorities—like official statistics—in our daily struggles. A reliance on tradition or cultural difference as the key delineator between Indigenous and Western methodologies also does little to help us disentangle these complexities and leaves us few tools for undertaking our analyses of modernity. Equally importantly, such analytical lenses remain focused solely in the direction of Indigenous communities, and in doing so handcuff our ability to undertake a task which should be central to any Indigenous research program: the deconstruction of Indigenous representations produced in and by dominant, settler, whitestream society (see the next section).

Additionally, there is a second set of factors at work here—our privilege and investment in academic fields. In the introduction we noted that the one thing that most scholars share in common, whether we aspire to be qualitative or quantitative in our orientation, is the fact that we are located in a university setting. To be sure, independent scholars exist, as do those located in government and non-government sectors of society. But a bulk of academic scholarship comes out of the academy. This is an important point to emphasize, because the privilege that we accrue from our position—the legitimacy our scholarship is given, the regard our interpretations are given, our ability to compete for funds to undertake said research, and our comparative privilege to travel the world to present our findings—separates us from others who make use of various kinds of Indigenous methods.

Thus, when we argue that, for example, storytelling constitutes a central element of Indigenous methodology, it becomes crucial to ask questions—and to be reflexive—about who is telling the story; who is in the audience, listening; what parts of the story are included, which are removed; what language it is told in; and what its effects are hoped to be. This is clearly part of a larger story about epistemology—what counts as truth and how we go about establishing it. But it is also a story about translation and about acknowledging the gaps between the kinds of power/truth produced in communities and those produced in the academy. The forms of investment, prestige, and expertise that exist in the academy mean that, by definition, stories told therein do not mean the same thing as those told in the community and, more importantly, do not have the same effects. For example, the stories of Leslie Marmon Silko (1981) that tell of her family and her Pueblo Indian community are not the same thing when they are analyzed in a literature thesis as when they are shared between family and community. Or when we write up the results of an elders discussion circle we cannot include all personal and cultural nuances and probably not even all the words that were spoken. The academic form, as do all forms of communication, places specific restrictions on which knowledge is conveyed and how. What is important is what this methodology represents—a form of academically legitimated Indigenous knowledge, and this, regardless of whether we use qualitative or quantitative means, is ground-breaking, orthodoxy breaking, and often brave scholarship. Similarly, with quantitative methodologies, while we may use different methods and report our results differently from qualitative scholars, what all those tables and coefficients represent is the legitimated entry of Indigenous knowledges into the academy by quantitative means.

In sum, we reiterate that Indigenous quantitative methodologies should not automatically be positioned as co-terminus with colonizer quantitative methodologies, despite the apparent similarity of their methods. To primarily define Indigenous quantitative methodologies in terms of their differences from colonizer settler frames underrates how the practice of quantitative research is distinctively shaped through an Indigenous methodology. Nonetheless, as outlined in the next section, Indigenous quantitative methodologies can be construed as challenging colonizer settler quantitative practices. Rather than gazing at the Indigenous, Indigenous quantitative methodologies use statistical methods to do the heavy lifting to clear intellectual space for exploring and analyzing what the colonizer settler gaze rarely acknowledges, the social situatedness of its own methodological choices.

The Purview of Indigenous Quantitative Methodologies

Indigenous quantitative methodologies reach well beyond the collection or use of statistical data about Indigenous peoples. We are knowers not just of Indigeneity, but of colonizing settler *whiteness* as well. Geonpul scholar Aileen Moreton-Robinson (2008: 85) argues that Indigenous peoples are well aware of and deeply steeped in knowledge about whiteness—how it operates, what it takes for granted, and its gaps, silences, and illogicalities. In many ways, we know the white colonizer/settler and the form and function of the white colonizer/settler state better than they know themselves. Despite the fact that "the knowledges we have developed are often dismissed as being implausible, subjective and lacking in epistemological integrity," Moreton-Robinson continues, "colonial experiences have meant that Indigenous people have been among the nation's most conscientious students of whiteness and racialization." Indeed, as Nicoll (2004: 21) states, "The fact that it is possible for Indigenous and/or non-white people to know [whites] demonstrates that epistemologies do exist outside the scopic regimes of Western modernity."

Situating Indigenous peoples as knowers within Indigenous quantitative methodology creates two unique research vantage points. First, as Indigenous people we know things about our Indigeneity that sit outside of the likelihood of Western disciplines to discover or analyze. In doing so, we challenge the otherwise unacknowledged power of colonizing settler whiteness in determining Indigenous subjectivity. As Moreton-Robinson (2008) also argues, within our first world nations Indigenous peoples are almost always situated as objects rather than subjects—not knowers, but *known*. Just as whiteness is often universalized to humanity, such positioning results in divisions regarding not only how valid knowledge is produced but also about who can produce it within colonially inscribed regimes of whiteness.[4]

The "unnamedness" of whiteness is the means through which dominant representations of Indigeneity are positioned as authentic, objective, and "true" at the expense of Indigenous knowledge production, either about ourselves or about others. For example, as argued in Chapter 1, in both Canada and Australia, Indigenous statistics are routinely paired with comparative data from the non-Indigenous population. The purpose is to demonstrate how far the Indigenous population deviates from the norm. That the vast majority of this comparative population are white Euro-Australians or Canadians is unnamed, and indeed, even the terminology 'non-Indigenous' actively refutes the idea that this group, as opposed to the Indigenous group, are raced at all. They are defined by the race they are not, not the race they are. Likewise, since the non-Indigenous norm is taken for granted, we rarely interpret the data in alternative ways—like, for example, comparing consumption levels or ecological footprints between

Indigenous and non-Indigenous populations, a comparison which would almost assuredly favor the Indigenous population.

Second, and equally important, Indigenous knowledge about whiteness can be used to "disrupt its claims to normativity and universality" (Moreton-Robinson 2008: 87). From this second vantage point colonizing white settler representations of Indigeneity—and of themselves—need to be challenged. Indigenous use of quantitative methodologies challenges the impression that such representations are logical *even* within their own epistemological premises. Colonized Indigenous first world nations' peoples have, through our centuries of interaction with our settler colonizing majorities, learned about dominant society on its own terms. As such we are uniquely positioned to critique it on its own terms. Indigenous quantitative methodologies, then, should and can provide empirical and theoretical insights into colonizer settler first world peoples' values and ways of being.

Indigenous methodology-framed research of our respective white peoples is unfortunately less widespread among Indigenous scholars than it should be. Moreton-Robinson's (2000) groundbreaking *Talkin up to the White Woman*, which qualitatively explored white feminist academics' understanding of race, is a notable exception, as is Vine Deloria's (1997) well known discussions of anthropologists in the U.S. context. Quantitative examples are even rarer (see Walter 2012 in Chapter 4). So long the object of study, for Indigenous scholars the terrain of the knowing research investigator on peoples other than our own feels unfamiliar, the responsibility large. If we move away from the relatively safe analytical ground of investigating ourselves to investigating our colonizing settler others, then we know we had better "get it right," for the position of research subject is also uncustomary for the non-Indigene. And as with any disruption of the traditional order of privilege the response to research subject/object table turning tends to be swift and harsh. As such, our research must be consciously framed and designed to be resistant to easy marginalization, if not outright dismissal.

This is where the strength of quantitative methodologies is most evident. The Western reverence for number and statistics as methodologically sound hard evidence valued over and above qualitative results reinforces the authority and the veracity of the reversal of the gaze research from ourselves to our colonizer settler populations. There is a belief in the veracity of statistical evidence within the political and policy realms of our nation-states institutions only infrequently extended to qualitative research, and, we argue, to Indigenous qualitative work in particular.

Indigenous quantitative research, therefore, presents Indigenous researchers with unique advantages. We can use the colonizer settler valuing of quantitative research to place our own quantitative research where it cannot be so easily rejected or excluded. Providing valid alternative visions of how colonizing settler peoples and societies operate breaks the current discursive paralysis and provides a healthy replacement for the everyday hegemonic uni-dimensional portraits of non-Indigenous/Indigenous relations we constantly encounter. Alternative interpretation, however, is not enough: as we speak to in the book's conclusion, Indigenization of the statistical cycle—including a role in the production of the categories themselves—is equally important (see Martin et al. 2002; Morphy 2007).

Indigenous quantitative research with predominantly colonizer settler subjects, however, must also be ethical in its approach. "Working ethically with white people" might sound facetious or at the very least ironic, but nonetheless remains an important issue. Having been treated unethically by white colonizer settler researchers ourselves is not an excuse to return the disfavor. As noted above, most colonizer settler peoples are epistemologically and ontologically unprepared to be the subject of Indigenous-framed research. The absolute normalcy of colonizer settler white privilege and its invisibility to its holders, combined with the unexpected resurgence of the Indigenous as the knowers and determiners of what is knowledge, can be an inflammatory and even incendiary mix. The response from those who become the subject of Indigenous study—possibly for the first time ever—can include anger and/or even rejection of the research as political and can lead to charges of reverse racism.

Thus, while Indigenous quantitative researchers must be prepared for dominant group power plays that attempt to silence our research and refute its epistemological legitimacy, we must also be mindful of the embeddedness of our subjects' colonizing settler epistemological norms. In Indigenous statistical space, colonizer settler peoples are the vulnerable ones. Their naivety in how their social positioning might emerge in highly unflattering ways can make such research the quantitative equivalent of shooting fish in a barrel. For example, in a recent co-authored article, Walter, Habibis, and Taylor (2011) argued that current Australian social work curricula and educational practices privilege white students and academics. One anonymous reviewer wrote: "I wondered who were the authors, regarding their cultural background, professional background (experience and qualifications) as this seemed to be relevant for me to know in the context of the paper." The article appeared to have caused the reviewer an "ontological shudder" (Mills 1997), and we can only surmise that he or she was seeking to establish if we were Aboriginal (one out of three), and by inference, if we were Aboriginal then perhaps we didn't have the experience or qualifications (we all did) to legitimize the piece. Our (accepted) response to the journal was that we thought this suggestion was inappropriate for a reviewer. So, we understand that our methodological practice and our results are likely to be epistemologically and ontologically disturbing, but their importance lies in their attempts to build a broader societal understanding of Indigenous standpoints, rather than to score points in the long-standing "blame game."

This second vantage point also allows us to escape from the confines of set-tler-imposed definitions of what it is to be an Indigenous scholar. For example, in challenging a book reviewer's criticism of her use of conventional academic rhetoric in formulating an argument, Moreton-Robinson (2006: 249) stated that the non-Indigenous reviewer appeared to be arguing that "Aborigines only speak with a colloquial flavour and, by implication, when we use conventional and or academic language we become less Aboriginal." Torres Strait Islander scholar Martin Nakata (1998: 5) argues similarly that "the issue for Indigenous scholars is one of how to speak back to the knowledges that have formed around what is perceived to be the Indigenous positions in the Coloniser settler 'order of things.'" As *Indigenous* scholars within academic relations of power, practi-tioners need to avail themselves of the symbolic power of, and launch part of their critique using, the very disciplinary knowledges that they are critiquing.

Conclusion

We conclude this chapter by arguing that first world Indigenous quantitative methodologies allow us to challenge methodological concepts and research practices that emphasize our *difference* at the expense of the *density* on full dis-play in our relationship with modernity. Moreover, the terms and the social relations encapsulated in our relationship to modernity comprise an important part of the density of contemporary Indigeneity. Writing off or ignoring these concepts is the analytical equivalent of burying our heads in the sand. *A prio-ris* don't simply evaporate if we fail to problematize them; rather, they niggle their way further into the foundations of discursive representations, insulating themselves from critique. Similarly, their dismissal creates a situation in which a dominant modality of knowledge production about Indigenous subjectivities is left to the labors of those who have little experience with or knowledge about our communities. As such, they "measure" us using methodologies that, though longstanding, carve out only narrow slices of our daily lives. In Chapters 4 and 5, we explore this issue in more practical detail, beginning with a discussion of *nayri kati* to explore Indigenous statistical space in Australia. We follow this with a discussion of similar issues in a Canadian context.

Notes

1 Also see Wacquant 1997.

2 For a general discussion regarding Canadian colonialism as seductive *as well as* oppressive, see Day 2000.

3 We should also balance the argument by stating the social fact that these power relations cut both ways, such that the constitution of our colonizing settler populations and institutions are also powerfully influenced and shaped by their long-standing interaction

with Indigeneity. As with first world colonized Indigenous peoples, the traditions, culture, identity, and knowledge systems of our respective colonizer settler peoples have also evolved via the process of colonization and settler state establishment and maintenance. Why is it that only Indigenous peoples' culture, knowledges, traditions, and identity are expected to remain unchanged?

4 I say similar in their apparent difference from whitestream normality, but I am certainly not conflating their subject positions. Moreton-Robinson argues elsewhere in a feminist context that the very prestige and privilege through which white, middle-class women are able to articulate their oppressions vis-à-vis their position in patriarchal societies as a universal experience is made possible by the unacknowledged dispossession of Indigenous territory. Aileen Moreton-Robinson, *Talkin up to the White Woman: Indigenous Women and Feminism*, University of Queensland Press, St. Lucia, 2000 (hereafter *Talkin Up to the White Woman*).

Chapter 4

nayri kati ("Good Numbers")
Indigenous Quantitative Methodology in Practice

Introduction

An Indigenous quantitative methodology is a quantitative methodology that embodies an Indigenous standpoint. In this chapter we define and demonstrate Indigenous quantitative methodology. Our aim is to make evident, first, how Indigenous quantitative methodologies can provide radically different insights into the statistical Indigene. Second, we show how Indigenous quantitative methodologies can provide insights into settler colonizing peoples and institutions, especially in their relationship to first world Indigenous peoples.

Our conceptualization of Indigenous quantitative methodology incorporates all the elements of a generic methodology defined in Chapter 2, but from an Indigenous frame. To demonstrate how this frame fundamentally changes the practice and processes of research our operationalization of a quantitative methodology, through the example of *nayri kati*,[1] is purposively constructed to reflect the embodiment of each of the constitutive elements of standpoint and the theoretical frame. The researcher's social position is first laid out, followed by an outline of the primary *nayri kati* theoretical framework. An explication of one of the three other standpoint tenets—epistemology, axiology, and ontology—is then aligned with the description of a specific research project. This format explains the philosophical underpinnings as well as the practice realities of research using an Indigenous quantitative methodology. The *nayri kati* examples, however, present only a hint of the potential and the capacity of Indigenous methodologies to reframe and re-invent Indigenous statistics.

Indigenous Statistics: A Quantitative Research Methodology by Maggie Walter and Chris Andersen,
82–110. © 2013 Left Coast Press, Inc. All rights reserved.

Defining Indigenous Quantitative Methodologies

Indigenous quantitative methodologies are methodologies within which the practices and the processes of the research are conceived and framed through an Indigenous standpoint. This definition aligns with our conceptualization of methodology in Chapter 2 and the discussion of the Indigenous methodology parameters in Chapter 3. As demonstrated in Figure 4.1, it is the researchers' standpoint that delineates the shared philosophical base that not only defines a quantitative methodology as an Indigenous methodology, but also situates that methodology within the broader Indigenous quantitative methodological paradigm.

Indigenous standpoint influences every aspect of the research methodology. The social position of Indigenous researchers differs politically, culturally, racially, and often economically from those of researchers from settler backgrounds. Using our extension of Bourdieu's (1984) concept of *habitus* to include race capital as well as social, economic, and cultural capital (Walter 2010c), the filters and frames through which Indigenous researchers make sense of our world as well as our own position within it result in an Indigenous-shaped

Figure 4.1: Conceptualization of an Indigenous Quantitative Methodology

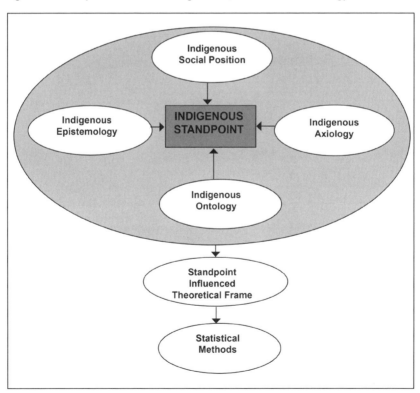

social position. Again, as argued in Chapter 2, our social position is not about individual choices. Our social position, inclusive of our capital relationalities, not only substantially prescribes our life circumstances, it forms the worldview through which we understand them. Thus, our research practice and how we approach research itself are molded by our social position. More particularly, while the makeup of social position will vary between Indigenous researchers, our similarities in racial, cultural, social, and economic capitals translate to shared understandings, values, and ways of seeing the world aligned with an Indigenous habitus. For us, the dominant settler population is the sometimes difficult to comprehend "them."

Epistemologically, this means that as Indigenous researchers what we regard as knowledge and how knowledges are prioritized is encapsulated within our Indigenous social and cultural framework. The epistemic consequences of Indigenous experiential existence will, therefore, differ from that derived from dominant settler social and cultural frameworks. For example, for Indigenous scholars, the Western canon of our respective disciplines is theoretically useful, but must be reframed and re-interpreted to be made sense within our research, as per how we have reframed Bourdieu's concept of social space to include racial capital. From these same frameworks, the axiological values we incorporate into how we do research will influence the practice and processes of that research. The topics we deem important and the way we go about investigating them will reflect Indigenous cultural, racial, political, and moral value systems rather than dominant Western mores. For example, our interactions with our Indigenous participants will be relational (Martin 2008; Wilson 2008) rather than transactional. Ontologically, Indigenous realities and ways of being vary significantly from settler understandings. From our various perspectives who we are, as Indigenous peoples and people, is far more than an individual statement of personality traits. This, of course, is the same for settler peoples, but the discourse of individualism operates as a cover for the majority of the settler population for what are equally strong, but dissimilar understandings of identity, cultural alignment, and belonging. It also follows that our theoretical frame will emanate from, and reflect, our standpoint.

In defining Indigenous quantitative methodologies, we stress the plurality: methodolog*ies*, not methodology. As we explained in the Introduction, while colonized first world Indigenous peoples share many attributes, such as our colonizing histories, our minority status, and our economic and political marginalization, we are not the same. Neither will Indigenous researchers from the same first world nation-states necessarily come from a single standpoint. This is not part of the essentialism debate. What we *are* arguing is that the quantitative methodologies of Indigenous people within and across colonized first world nation-states will have points of similarity along their social position, epistemological, axiological, and ontological continuums. This will be manifest in the questions we pose, the answers we seek, the way we seek those answers, and the guiding theoretical frames that align with our standpoint. These parallel points are what categorize Indigenous quantitative methodologies as a distinctive paradigm. They form the demarcation line between Indigenous and colonizer settler quantitative methodological paradigms. Keep these caveats— that is, the differences as well as the similarities between first world colonized Indigenous peoples and the differences as well as the similarities between first world colonizing settler peoples—in mind when reading the next two chapters. For example, in *nayri kati*, standpoint is developed from within the Australian nation-state from the perspective of Australian Aboriginal peoples and contains other aspects unique to the researcher. We ask the reader to look past these specifics to garner a more general portrait of how an Indigenous quantitative methodology can be conceptualized, operationalized, and practiced.

The central message of these examples is that they represent research that is framed through and within an Indigenous standpoint. It is not that non-Indigenous researchers could not physically do this work, just as it was possible for male researchers to have undertaken much of the groundbreaking work of feminist researchers in the 1970s and the 1980s. It is just far less likely that they would do so. The social position, epistemological, axiological, and ontological frame of settler researchers (or male researchers in the case of feminist researchers) is not conducive to envisioning the research and its processes and practices in the same way as envisioned by Indigenous researchers. Standpoint dictates research practice.

nayri kati: An Indigenous Quantitative Methodology

Meaning "good numbers" in the *palawa* Tasmanian Aboriginal language, *nayri kati* encompasses much more than a name. As philosophers such as Wittgenstein (1974) and Foucault (1972) have argued convincingly, language is neither a neutral nor transparent medium; it shapes not only what we say but what we can think and how we understand our social world. Language creates boundaries around our discursive capacities. Naming this quantitative methodology from my own Indigenous language, therefore, is more than artifice. It aligns the methodology with my[2] standpoint, proclaiming the influence of Indigeneity on how I see the world and, in turn, the project of quantitative research. Similarly, the reference to good numbers indicates that dominant modes of doing statistics do not necessarily operate in the interests of Indigenous peoples. As detailed in Chapter 1, the dominant terrain of Indigenous statistics operates in ways that entrench political, cultural, and social marginalization for Indigenous communities and, conversely, entrench the privileged positions and viewpoints of the settler majority.

nayri kati encapsulates two key methodological purposes. The first is to generate statistical data through an Indigenous lens that:

1. privileges Indigenous voices, knowledges, and understandings;
2. does not take Euro-Australians or their accompanying value systems as the unacknowledged norm;
3. does not take a presumption of Indigenous deficit as its starting point.

The second purpose is to challenge the hegemony of Indigenous statistical practice by exposing the standpoint from which it operates. This standpoint is currently obscured under a mantle of presumed neutrality. These two purposes are manifest in the following demonstration of *nayri kati* and are articulated in each of the examples of *nayri kati* in practice.

naryi kati Standpoint

naryi kati Social Location

How a researcher perceives the world in which his or her research topic is located is inevitably, but complexly, influenced by the filters and frames of life experiences and social, cultural, economic, and personal identity location. The personal, political, cultural, and the academic become entwined. We are not just researchers; we are *socially located* researchers. This applies to Indigenous researchers as much as it does to those from other racial and/or cultural backgrounds. As Indigenous researchers from colonized first world Indigenous peoples, we share an Indigenous lived reality. But our experiences of Indigeneity are not identical, nor are our other life and social positions. In Australia, Indigenous women's life experiences and circumstances differ from those of Indigenous men; being a salt water person is not the same as being a desert person; being *pakana* is not the same as being Yolngu (an Australian Aboriginal people from northeastern Australia); being an older person means my perspectives and priorities are different from those of a younger person; and I have lived through, and been influenced by, different life circumstances and social and historical actualities. None of these dimensions of the experiences of Indigeneity accord directly with the Indigenous lived reality of being Māori, or Native Hawaiian, or Native American, although the similarity of the logic of our nation-states' rationalities ensure some similarities. *nayri kati* is therefore influenced by my social, cultural, and economic location as well as my Indigenous identity, my life history, and that of my Aboriginal nation.

For researchers, explicating our social position can be a double-edged sword. On one hand, spelling out who we are, who we think we are, and why provides insight across the multiple facets of our lives, and life biography allows us an understanding of why we are the scholars and the researchers that we are. In illuminating and often surprising ways, how the intersections of biology, class location, biography, and history have influenced our understanding of both ourselves and the social world can be cathartic and reassuring. The process also refutes the capacity to hide within what Mills (1997) refers to as "epistemologies of ignorance." While specifically referring to racial epistemologies of ignorance whereby the cognitive model of the dominant Euro majority precludes self-transparency and any genuine understanding of racial social realities, epistemologies of ignorance which preclude self-transparency and a genuine understanding of social realities and the (white) world which they themselves both create and sustain, can also be linked to the other key social forces of class and gender. We are not, and cannot be, separated from these positions and lived realities when we research. We are as embedded in our social worlds as our research subjects, and we embody our social position in how we approach, understand, and do research.

On the other hand, explicating our social position publicly can make us vulnerable as both people and researchers. This is particularly the case for Indigenous researchers. The social position of others to whom we are revealing can mean that what we reveal can actually further our construction and essentialization as the Indigene, an object of curiosity, diminishing our scholarship in the process. For example, while now being very clear about how I understand my social position when I present my work, I consciously resist public discussion of my personal background as part of that presentation. This resistance emerges from a scenario, faced by many Indigenous scholars, of being asked personal identity or generic Indigenous questions rather than scholarship related questions by conference or other audiences.

For example, I was once asked after a presentation on the terrain of race relations in Australia if I could explain why some local Aboriginal people (a community of which I was not a member) were unwilling to participate in an event he was trying to organize. I am also frequently asked to tell the audience about my Aboriginal background. Publicly, I am firmly polite that that is not the topic of my presentation, please ask a relevant question. Privately, I am irritated at what I perceive as a racialized affront and a white privilege power play, although the asker may or may not have perceived it as such. Asking a personal rather than a presentation-related question is tantamount to a public refusal to recognize my scholarship. Such a question indicates that, for the asker, Indigeneity trumps scholarship. I am being defined by race in a way that those who are Euro-Australian never are, and a consequence of that definition is that the questioner is reasserting his or her dominant racial positioning. The assumption of a right of entry to the personal also reduces me from a peer to an object of voyeurism.

Again, I regard this as a manifestation of white privilege, although I know that the requester is often unaware that I might find the question offensive. I see it as an attempt to reassert the traditional subject-object order non-Indigenous/Indigenous relations (Indigenous audiences never ask me these sorts of questions). Regardless of my qualifications or the strength of my scholarship I have to be the object, not the subject analyser. Can you imagine a male white American historian presenting on the American war of independence being asked to describe how being Euro-American had impacted on his life and how he practiced his culture. But in the interest this book's standpoint focus, I will here contextualize my research standpoint through a description of my social position.

nayri kati Indigenous Context of Social Location

I am a descendant of the *trawlwoolway* people of northeastern Tasmania. This identity and heritage is heavily influenced by the colonizing history of Tasmania and its Aboriginal peoples. When the British established their first colonial settlement in Tasmania in 1803, it is estimated that the island was already occupied by between 4,000 and 10,000 Tasmanians, grouped across the island in nine nations (Ryan 1995). Unlike other Indigenous lands they colonized, such as those now situated within the United States, Canada, and New Zealand, the British made no formal treaties with Australian Aboriginal peoples. Instead, they chose to interpret those peoples' hunter-gatherer lifestyle to mean that no recognizable rule of law existed. Under the British legal doctrine of *terra nullius* (un-owned land) the land was claimed and occupied in the name of the British Crown without recourse or recompense to its population.

The overt purpose of British colonization was to provide a dumping ground for the convicted felons overcrowding English jails and other penal institutions. And although initially limited to small areas of Tasmania, the first killings of Aboriginal people took place within the first weeks of the British presence. European diseases also quickly took their toll on those living in proximity to the penal colonies and supporting townships. An additional menace was the sealers who came to plunder the large fur seal populations of the islands off the northeast coast of Tasmania. By the early nineteenth century these men were regularly kidnapping Aboriginal women as concubines and workers, prized for their seal catching and skinning skills.

By the mid 1820s, an influx of British settler colonists moved what had been sporadic contact violence to all out war. The "black wars" saw regular military expeditions against the Tasmanians and growing public demands by the colonists for something to be done about the "Aboriginal problem" (Bonwick 1969). The failure of military means to subdue the Tasmanians saw the colonial authorities moved to conciliatory ploys. In exchange for relocating to off-shore islands, the Tasmanians were promised they would be free to live an unfettered life. With a population now reduced to just hundreds, the Tasmanians agreed. The promise of freedom was never kept. Exile was captivity and confinement under colonial authority in the purpose built establishment at Wybalenna (Black Man's Houses) on Flinders Island (Reynolds 1995).

At Wybalenna, unhealthy living conditions and despair resulted in on-going illness and early death among the Tasmanians. Numbers continued to plummet. By 1841, when my matriarch Woretemoeteyenner was released into the care of her daughter Dalrymple Briggs in mainland Tasmania (the only Tasmanian ever released from Wybalenna), only forty-seven other traditional Aboriginal people remained alive. By 1876, the last of the original Tasmanians, Trucanini, was also dead.[3] The only survivors were the progeny of the sealer-kidnapped women who escaped the initial roundup. I, and the vast majority of other contemporary Aboriginal Tasmanians, am descended from these women and their captors.

For the colonists, the extinction of the Tasmanians, supported by theories of social Darwinism, was portrayed as a regrettable but unavoidable consequence of colonization. It was (is) as if the Tasmanians had merely faded away rather than being hunted, shot, and held in disease-ridden captivity until they were all dead. Myths of the Tasmanians as the occupiers of the lowest rung on the Chain of Being also circulated and bodily remains were much sought after by British, European, and North American museums, universities, and other seats of Western learning. The skeleton of Trucanini, against her express wishes, was disinterred and put on public display at the Tasmanian Museum until the mid 1950s. And perhaps as the ultimate extinction, throughout most of the twentieth century it was official Tasmanian government policy that there were no Aboriginal Tasmanians. Tasmanian descendants, such as myself, were told we didn't exist. The official and the actual were of course very different. The Aboriginality of many Tasmanian families was well known by themselves and their neighbours, and Aboriginal children were specifically targeted for welfare removal from their families.

This all changed in the 1970s when Aboriginal political activism led to official (re)recognition of the Tasmanian population. In 1976, Trucanini's cremated remains were scattered in the D'Entrecasteaux Channel as per her original wishes by Tasmanian descendants, and we began and continue our efforts to have the stolen remains of our people returned for respectful burial in their homelands. Small parcels of land, including the Wybalenna site, have now been returned to the community, and an official state apology for the forced removal of Aboriginal children was made in 2006, along with the establishment of a compensation fund. Despite these advances, the Aboriginal population, now numbering over 10,000, remains the poorest and most socially disadvantaged group in Tasmania.

The Translation of Social Location to Research Methodology

What does all this mean for my social position? My age means I know what it is to be disallowed my Aboriginal identity, simultaneously with that same

Aboriginality being a pejorative social marker. My understandings are also consolidated through my family's involvement in the political and functional revival of Aboriginal Tasmania in the mid 1970s and my own early employment at a then fledgling Aboriginal community legal and social support organization. Coming from a large, poor family contributed to my leaving school early without qualifications. As such, my journey into academia and research has been a long, arduous one, undertaken as an adult and combined with family and other paid work responsibilities. Yes, I now fit the profile, socio-economically, of being middle class, but such class status is most definitely "late onset." It is also one in which my fit, in terms of my social and cultural capital, remains tenuous.

This social position obviously affects my understanding of my place in the world as a person and as a researcher. It means I am highly sensitive to race as a social construct and as a lived reality, and tend to perceive the key Australian racial binary of whiteness and Indigeneity in ways usually not open to my non-Indigenous (mostly white) academic colleagues. For my scholarship and research these sensitivities foster my intrigue with the politics of race and how race, particularly whiteness, is performed to create the "everyday" of Australian social space, in contrast with Indigeneity. This intellectual prism energizes my fascination with the phenomenon of power, especially as it pertains to the relations between the colonizing state, the white settler majority, and co-resident Aboriginal populations. The social forces of gender and class and their intersection with race also fall under this scholarly purview. In the following sections, this social position is clearly reflected within *nayri kati's* conceptualization and practice.

nayri kati Theoretical Framework

In our methodology map, the research theoretical framework flows from standpoint, and this is how *nayri kati* should be conceptualized. Its exposition is placed here to demonstrate how theoretical framework embodies the *nayri kati* standpoint *and* how this is reflected in the research examples. The major theoretical and conceptual frame used within *nayri kati* is my theory of the domain of Aboriginality. This is a theoretical frame that has been evolving for me over a number of years (see Moreton-Robinson and Walter 2010; Walter 2009). My theory is aligned within the broader critical race relations paradigm and has power as its central theoretical concern. It seeks to provide a theoretical platform for understanding how power is used in micro and macro social arrangements and interactions to bolster the claims and interests of the privileged that are the dominant Euro-Australian population, culture, political, and economic interests. *naryi kati's* theoretical frame, then, is informed by the terrain of race relations and the position of Indigenous people in Australian society, in relation to the dominant group. Its focus is the way power embeds this disadvantaged and privileged positioning via the everyday racial landscape of present and past social-structural reality.

The relationship and power interactions of the Australian nation-state towards its Indigenous peoples are also theoretically central. This conceptual grid can be figuratively and theoretically mapped as the domain of Aboriginality.[4] Within this context, the term Aboriginality does not denote identity. Rather, the term encapsulates the lived experience of being Indigenous in Australia in relation to the settler population and the broader impact of these power relations on individual and group life chances and life options. The domain is multifaceted, with intersecting layers, but components can be identified within thematic clusters.

Cluster 1: Material Poverty

Cluster 1, material poverty, incorporating our comparative socio-economic position, is the one most readily identified Indigenous positioning, especially for non-Indigenous Australians. Indeed, as argued in the Introduction, it forms a central platform, based on statistics, on how the Indigenous people in this country are seen by the Euro-Australian majority, the nation-state, and some-times by ourselves. What this cluster indicates first is that, regardless of region, background, urban or remote location, Indigenous peoples are always the most disadvantaged across all socio-economic indicators (AIHW 2011a). But mate-rial poverty is more than just contemporary socio-economic position. Material poverty must also be understood as stemming from Indigenous exclusion from a relative share of Australian society's resources and opportunities. It is also about the embedded over-privilege of the majority and the normalization of this privilege in Australian society. Our exclusion from resources and oppor-tunities is historic as well as contemporary. The result is the second item: an inherited socio-economic deprivation accruing and accumulating across and into the life chances of Indigenous individuals, families, and communities. This material poverty marker can be contrasted with how privilege accrues and accumulates across the life chances of settler populations, especially those granted our dispossessed lands. Additionally, not only are Indigenous people poor, but we are explicitly and implicitly excluded from the right to any mate-rial privilege. Non-Aboriginal Australia expects Aboriginal people to be poor, and any notion of Indigenous prosperity appears to be resented (Walter 2008). Equality, in non-Indigenous terms, does not seem to extend to an equitable share of privilege.

Cluster 2: Absences and Omissions

A cluster of four absences encapsulates the normalized Australian omission of the Indigenous. First and second, Indigenous people are spatially and social-ly separated from non-Indigenous Australia. Over two-thirds of Aboriginal people live in regional and metropolitan urban areas, yet Indigenous lives remain separated in almost all spheres from non-Indigenous lives within the same geographic location. Most non-Indigenous Australians' lives are totally disconnected from Indigenous people or realities. As shown in the research example later in this chapter, the vast majority of Euro-Australians do not mix regularly with an Aboriginal people, and census mapping of the urban places where over three-quarters of Aboriginal people reside shows that even when we live in the same cities, we don't live in the same spaces, physically or socially (Atkinson, Taylor, and Walter 2010; Walter 2008). Third and fourth, these absences are magnified by the physical and symbolic absence of Indigenous Australia/ns from the political realm and spheres of influence. This extends to the nation-state's concept of itself and the business of state. Except as a directly problematic topic, Indigenous people as citizens are missing in conceptions of everyday Australian life, and these absences are unremarked and deemed unremarkable in contemporary mainstream Australian culture. The one place we do appear is as culturally appropriated icons. Our dancers, our didgeridoo players, and our traditional cultural ceremonies are regularly called upon to provide spectacles of Australianness, especially for visiting dignitaries and high level public and political events, but the spaces for our contemporary realties remain firmly restricted.

Cluster 3: Burden of Disregard

The social and spatial separations of Indigenous absences allow for non-Indigenous/Indigenous relations to be pejoratively based. Indigenous Australia carries what Sheehan (personal communication 2007) refers to as the "burden of disregard," the normalization of disrespect towards Aboriginal peoples that permeates everyday Australian life. Within our social institutions, if we are represented at all, it is as an equity group. This allows the core business of the institutions to be conducted outside any regard for the specific needs of their Indigenous constituents or, more problematically, the benefits such engagement could bring. And while most Australians are horrified at the idea of being cast as racist, a constant patter of casual and usually thoughtless denigration of Aboriginal people and culture is threaded into the fabric of the nation's conversations. It is heard everywhere: in taxis, in the hairdresser's, in restaurants.[5] The widely discussed "deficits" and "inadequacies" of Indigenous people, culture, and lifestyles also provide a circular rationale for Indigenous inequality. Our inequality is deemed the consequence of our inability to live "normal lives." Moreover, the huge inequities in life chances are perceived through an on-going, individually and community invasive, judgemental, but socially remote, media and public scrutiny. Despite our making up only 2.5 percent of the total Australian story there is not a week that does not include an

Indigenous story in Australian mainstream media, and the vast majority of these focus on aspects such as poverty, alcohol consumption, lack of attendance at schooling, and the list goes on. And while many of these stories are sympathetic to the Indigenous plight, they also embed negative stereotypes.

Cluster 4: Ongoing Dispossessions

Categorizing dispossessions encompass more than loss of land or culture or traditional knowledges. Colonization has meant most Indigenous people are

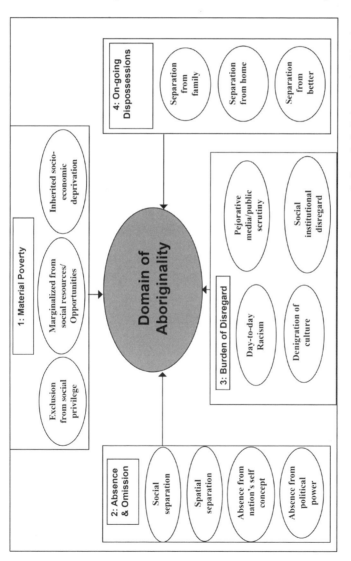

Figure 4.2: The Domain of Aboriginality: The Terrain of an Indigenous Life in Australia

Source: An earlier iteration of this figure appeared in Walter 2008 and Moreton-Robinson and Walter 2009

separated from country, and claims to country thus remain perpetually subservient to the entitlement demands of non-Indigenous Australia. In my own case of Tasmanian pakana peoples, lack of ongoing physical inhabitation of the traditional country from which we were forcibly dispossessed has also meant that our identity as Indigenous peoples has also been consistently challenged. And for a significant proportion of Indigenous people, the legacy of dispossessions also means a separation in some shape or form from family. Yet, perhaps the most penetrating dispossession is in the expectation of a poor deal. The lived experience of this generation and those who came before is too often founded on ill-health, substance abuse, and the early and pointless deaths of family members. The result is that dramatically circumscribed life chances and a hard daily reality have become a normalized aspect of Indigenous life. For many the weight of today's difficulties means a soul destroying dispossession from hope for a different future, for individuals or for communities (see Dudgeon et al. 2012 for a searing account of how lack of hope, and lack of self worth emanating from the burden and disregard, absence and omissions, and dispossessions damage Indigenous peoples).

nayri kati Epistemology

As detailed in Chapter 1, epistemology concerns what is counted as knowledge, who can and who cannot be knowledgeable, and the hierarchy of how knowledges are valued. In traditional (Western) quantitative methodologies the epistemic designation of knowers and knowledge is value-ranked along a culturally, racially, and socially laden continuum. Hierarchies of knower and knowledge by subject/object position exist in which the usual position of the Indigene is limited to data source, even if it is increasingly fashionable to "consult" this data source. The epistemic boundaries of *nayri kati* challenge these established hierarchies of knower and knowledge. *naryi kati* epistemically places race, and relatedly power, at the center of its approach, placing the Indigene as the observer of these phenomena.

The vast majority of existing Indigenous related quantitative research in Australia (and other colonized first world nations), as detailed in Chapter 1, is research conducted by non-Indigenous researchers on data collected from Indigenous peoples. These studies use national omnibus surveys, such as the national census, or administrative collections, such as birth, death, and marriage records, or, in some cases, specifically collected data, such as that from the National Aboriginal and Torres Strait Islander Surveys (NATSIS), which were run in 1994, 2002, 2008, and are due again in 2014. The prevailing methodology for these researches is Western quantitative methodology, with Euro-Australian dominant knowledges shaping how the research is done. The question or questions that the research addresses are conceived and developed by non-Indigenous, predominantly Euro-Australian entities and are usually predicated on the primary objective of measuring what are defined as Indigenous problems. For example, census, health administrative collection and NATSIS data are all used to provide the results for the biennial national report—*The Social and Health Wellbeing of Australia's Aboriginal and Torres Strait Islander Peoples*—produced by the Australian Institute of Health and Welfare. In almost all of these studies (see next section for an example of an exception) Aboriginal and Torres Strait Islander people are the objects of the research, providing data whose subject, level, type, analysis, and interpretation have been developed by non-Indigenous expert knowers.

In deliberate and direct contrast to this approach, within *nayri kati*, even when some of the same data sources are utilized, Indigenous knowledges and Indigenous knowers are prioritized. This methodological practice entails overtly including Indigenous voices and knowledges in all "knowledge related" aspects of the research process. That is, Indigenous knowledges and conceptual and practical understandings are the lens through which research knowledge is revealed. This epistemic hierarchy also forestalls the restriction of Indigenous quantitative research to Indigenous subjects.

Research Example 1: Indigenous Knowers and Evaluators

Indigenous participation in higher education has long been a subject of the higher education sector, government, and policy interest in Australia and other first world settler nations. Under the Howard Government (1996–2007), Indigenous education was considered such a high priority that a report on all aspects, including Indigenous higher education, was delivered annually to the national parliament. Each of these reports (2001–2008) was written by non-Indigenous bureaucrats from the responsible government department. Their common format was to aggregate statistics provided by individual universities, highlight points from the individual university Indigenous Education Statements (IES), and intersperse these statistics with vignettes about, and photos of, various Indigenous student centers. The general message of each of the reports was that although progress was slower than desired, progress was being made. For example, the 2006 report (DEEWR 2008: 129) concludes regarding Indigenous student enrolment that:

> after a decline in 2005, overall 2006 Indigenous enrolments return to 2001–2004 levels. Especially noteworthy is the increase in participation in higher level courses and the rapid decline in students undertaking Enabling and other non-degree courses.

In 2011 I was the quantitative researcher on a study which also had as its topic Aboriginal and Torres Strait Islander participation in higher education

(Moreton-Robinson, Walter, Singh, and Kimber 2011). This research was commissioned by the panel of *The Review of Higher Education Access and Outcomes for Aboriginal and Torres Strait Islander People*. Our brief was to evaluate the public Australian universities' performances in relation to Indigenous governance. This study, similar to the previous national reports, also used departmental statistics and the publicly available annual Indigenous Education Statements issued by each university. Our selection of the same data sources was a deliberate strategy to forestall delegitimization of our analysis by labelling it political or activist. Epistemologically, for this project, however, Indigenous researchers were the observers, not non-Indigenous bureaucrats. And it was Indigenous conceptual and practical understandings that formed the knowledge lens through which university Indigenous governance was evaluated. The process and practice of this research shows how this epistemological positioning shaped the research design, data analysis, and interpretation of results.

First, we conceptualized governance to encompass Aboriginal and Torres Strait Islander participation and direct influence on university executive functions and the regulation of Aboriginal and Torres Strait Islander participation in higher education. Regulation refers to the strategies, programs and objectives to increase Indigenous outcomes including embedding Indigenous knowledges within universities' operations.

We then translated this conceptualisation into two research questions:

1. How well do universities incorporate Aboriginal and Torres Strait Islander participation into their structures of governance?

2. How efficacious is the governance of programs to build Aboriginal and Torres Strait Islander student and staff participation and cultural presence within universities?

Our theoretical framework, customary management practice, also deliberately drew on standard (Western) management theory. Customary management practice was defined as per Collier (1998) as practices, processes, activities, and monitoring systems organizations implement in any area of major activity. My role was to quantitatively analyze the departmental statistics on Indigenous students, undergraduate and graduate, as well as staff numbers, and to devise a way of numerically evaluating data from the content analysis of the Indigenous Education Statements on Indigenous staff and student participation and participation in university governance undertaken by other members of the research team.

Rather than statistical aggregation, we purposely kept the data disaggregated by university. Aggregation can be a statistical decontextualizing device that distances data from the people and institutions whose actions, or lack of, contribute to creating the thing these data are measuring. I further devised a numerical scale whereby the performance of each of the thirty-seven Australian universities could be evaluated across the dimensions of Indigenous governance presence, Indigenous undergraduate and post-graduate student access, and attainment and Indigenous staff employment. First, we accorded scores to each institution based on what the IES content analysis indicated about the level of that university's policies, objectives, targets, key performance indicators, and formal evaluation of its Indigenous participation activities. Student and staff enrolment and employment statistics were also analyzed and scored by comparing actual numbers with what the numbers would be if Indigenous staff and students were represented at Australian Bureau of Statistics state-based Indigenous population figure rates. For the governance and cultural competence measures we also included a score based on whether the university reported an Indigenous appointment at the senior management level.

Our scale allowed us to rate individual universities and then rank them by order of overall performance. Our results indicated that two-thirds of Australian universities recorded total scores of less than 50 points out of a possible 100. A reduced anonymized version of this rating/ranking is represented in Table 4.1.

For this study, the Indigenous standpoint of knowers has significant epistemic consequences. How were these manifested? First, in contrast to most similar studies, the universities were our objects of study, not our knowers. We evaluated their performance against publicly available data, just as the bureaucrats had done, but interrogated those data in a very different manner. It was a critical analysis framed through an Indigenous world view. Second, our Indigenous scholar knowledge informed our conceptualization, question generation, and operationalization of the key concept, Indigenous governance. Together, these knowledges allowed us to evaluate aspects of governance more broadly and in ways more in tune with our own understandings of sector connections. Third, by individually rating and ranking universities we showed not only that progress is slow but in what spaces and places. We brought a relational accountability of specific universities to their Indigenous communities into the analysis for the first time. The fact that some universities, albeit a minority, were achieving a rating of above 50 points also foreclosed the standard responses that the sector is committed to raising levels of Indigenous governance. For example, each of these universities has Indigenous clauses in their industrial awards, and each talks about their commitment to Indigenous employment and leadership (NTEU 2012). Our results, however, clearly demonstrate that while some universities are taking active steps to increase Indigenous participation, others remain in the "committed to being committed" category. The fact that some universities are making gains also refuted the common argument reported by our colleagues at universities around the nation that they, the universities, were committed to greater Indigenous participation, but that the Indigenous community was hard to engage.

Table 4.1: Indigenous Governance Scores of Australian Universities

University	Students Access & Attainment 40%	Academic Professional Staff 30%	Governance Engagement 30%	Total Score 100
University a	26	17	21	64
University b	26	30	7	63
University c	19	25	14	55
University d	18	21	14	53
University e	21	26	3	50
University f	17	20	11	48
University g	18	19	5	41
University h	13	22	3	38
University i	14	16	6	36
University j	9	16	9	34
University k	13	18	2	33
University l	7	15	10	32
University m	16	12	2	30
University n	7	8	12	27
University o	7	14	5	26
University p	9	13	3	25

Source: Derived from Moreton-Robinson, Walter, Singh, and Kimber 2011

Fourth, and most critically, by asking different questions of the same data, the problematic of low and only minimally increasing Indigenous participation in the higher education sector was situated within the individual university and the sector, not with Aboriginal staff or centers. We found that those universities who had best defined policies, backed by clear objectives, targets, key performance indicators, and on-going evaluation of these, were also those with the highest number of Indigenous enrolments, staff, and Indigenous participation in governance. This correlation was not related to chance. Clearly, university leaders who back their commitment with action achieved better results.

Finally, the power of the data is demonstrated by how this report has been used. As expected, the first response by a number of university hierarchies was to question our methods, a response quickly blunted by reference to our data sources and theoretical frame. More importantly, it has been widely picked up by Indigenous higher education leaders and others throughout the sector and used both to commend their universities and as evidence for the need for university-wide changes in how Indigenous business is done.

Aiming for an Indigenous Epistemological Fit

In research where Indigenous people are also the subject of the research, the *nayri kati* epistemic prioritization of Indigenous voices goes further. Most critically, the information sought from Indigenous subjects and the "for what purpose" must be developed using Indigenous knowledges and understandings. This does not preclude the involvement of non-Indigenous researchers in the work, but in the hierarchy it is Indigenous knowers and knowledge that take the dominant position. As the Indigenous knowers framing the research and the Indigenous subjects of research are rarely the same people, this epistemological rule does not guarantee epistemic fit. Unless we are working with our own individual Indigenous communities, we are also outsiders. And as the literature on insider/outsider debate makes clear (see Acker 2000; Adler and Adler 1987), being an insider is still problematic when determining the relationship and most appropriate interaction between a researcher and the researched. This positioning can be even more problematic in Indigenous research given the family and kin relationships involved. But it does provide a broader scope for symmetry. It does lessen the power differential between the researcher and the researched from that common in the dominant methodology of research on Indigenous people, which even within the major data collection agencies tends to restrict the Indigenous presence to controlled "consultation."

nayri kati also recognizes and incorporates existing philosophical work on Indigenous epistemologically. As our scholars cogently argue (see Martin 2008; Rigney 2001; West 1998), knowledges located within research are not, ever, the property of the researcher. For Indigenous peoples worldwide, knowing and seeking knowledge is never a solo enterprise. It also cannot be separated from our understanding of who knowers can be—that not all knowers can be knowers of all things, and not all things can be known (see Martin 2008; Wilson 2008). Knowledge, therefore, cannot be discovered, or owned. But it can be revealed and shared, and the how, by whom, to whom, from what perspective and for what purpose this revealing occurs is one of the facets that delineate an Indigenous methodology.

nayri kati Axiology

Research cannot be a value free zone, and all quantitative methodologies are value infused entities. Critically, the decisions we make about the research process, from the inception of the research idea to its final interpretation and dissemination, are not spontaneous. A key shaper of these decisions is the researcher and/or his or her controlling institution's value systems, even when—perhaps *especially* when—these are unacknowledged. The question asked in Chapter 2 of how much a researcher's and/or his or her funders' value systems can be disentangled from his or her research practice, therefore, is also valid for Indigenous quantitative researchers. For *nayri kati*, the answer stems from personal values and judgement systems embedded in my particular milieu: I recognize the unattainability of the holy grail of research objectivity but also recognize the imperative of always aiming towards it.

Other value systems, however, are consciously included. *nayri kati*'s explicit axiological frame incorporates and prioritizes relevant Indigenous value systems. The primary value is that the research is tangibly operating for, and in, Indigenous interests. The first axiological infused decision, therefore, is whether the research should be undertaken at all. For example, research framed from a model of Indigenous deficit outlined in Chapter 1 actively undermines the Indigenous position across colonizer settler nations. Other research can be less malignant but no more axiologically valid. For example, the seemingly intransigent socio-economically deprived position of many first world Indigenous peoples can lead to quantitative research undertaken without any pre-ordained Indigenous benefit or purpose. That is, research for research's sake. Collecting data on an Indigenous community's housing situation, for instance, without that research being directly tied to the possibility of remedial housing funding is harmful in its lack of purpose and its imposition of a research burden. A better topic, if you could get the funding, would be an evaluation of the efficacy of housing social services for Indigenous people. Alternatively, research that might ostensibly be in Indigenous peoples' interests does not always automatically reflect Indigenous value systems. This lack of fit can be very frustrating to non-Indigenous research commissioners or designers who cannot understand why there is resistance to some of their plans when they are manifestly trying to improve the social position of Aboriginal and Torres Strait Islander people. What is primarily at issue here is not Indigenous value systems but the non-recognition of settler value systems, by those that hold them, as actually being value systems.

An example of how these barriers and clashes of value systems can be successfully mediated is found in the research processes of the on-going Australian Longitudinal Study of Indigenous Children (LSIC 2005). This large scale panel study of nearly 2,000 study children from around Australia took four years to move from design to implementation. From the beginning the project has been overseen in all its elements by a steering committee co-chaired by leading Aboriginal and Torres Strait Islander researchers. The rest of the committee is made up of Indigenous and non-Indigenous (nearly all Euro-Australian) researchers and the implementing department officials and project team. The first misfit of values was over how the recruitment of families would be conducted. From an Indigenous value frame, research with these families could not proceed without their full engagement. This was much more than signed consent. It meant that any participants fully understood what they were committing to and what the project would mean for their family and the broader Indigenous population, were fully in agreement with the philosophy and aims of the study, and felt the project to be tangibly in their interests. In short, trusting relationships had to be built, and the building of those relationships had to conform to what our Indigenous families and communities regarded as the appropriate way to build a relationship. The non-Indigenous researchers who had worked with Indigenous peoples were also supportive of this need.

The steering committee needed to convince, and then convince again, the funding department that we could not begin surveying until we were assured that the study communities and families were fully informed and in support. The minimal informing and consent processes common for Euro-Australian participant survey research were not consistent with Indigenous values. More critically, their deployment would likely render the research ineffective—the success of the longitudinal survey is all about the success of recruiting participants, and standard Western approaches could not just be translated to this study. Instead, we needed repeated, not one-off, community visits from study staff, on-going contact with our families, the employment of local Indigenous data collection staff where possible, and a start date for data collection that built in these requirements. To the funding department's credit they made the axiological transition and put in the extra time, training, and visits required, along with coping with the extra expenses such consulting work required. We are now collecting Wave 8 data in what is proving to be a high participant retention study.

Even now new axiological problems emerge. The very success of the survey has led to many other agencies and government bodies requesting survey items be included. The steering committee mostly resists these additions. Yes, the items might be interesting, but unless they fall within the original purview of the intent of the survey—exploring how Indigenous children grow up strong—then they are outside of the agreement we made with our families and communities. We do not have their permission.

Research Example 2: Exploring Non-Indigenous Values

Projects that reflect Indigenous values and operate perceptibly in Indigenous interests do not necessarily involve research on, or with, Indigenous peoples. *nayri kati*'s axiological frame can also be applied in research based on colonizer settler Australian responses; in essence, evaluating non-Indigenous value systems through an Indigenous value frame. This practice is demonstrated by my inclusion of three sets of Indigenous-related items within the 2007 Australian Survey of Social Attitudes (AuSSA) (Walter 2012). The AuSSA survey is a mail out/mail back survey that canvasses the attitudes of a national representative group of Australians on items as varied as government priorities and abortion (AuSSA 2007). The 2007 survey had 2,699 respondents, around 94 percent of whom were from European or Euro-Australian backgrounds.

My topic was contemporary race relations as evidenced through the attitudes of non-Indigenous Australians towards Indigenous issues. The topic emerges from my interest in race related inequality and seeks to apply an Indigenous lens in making sense of the unequal Indigenous positioning in the broader Australian society. From this perspective research on Indigenous inequality is intricately entwined with its opposite, non-Indigenous privilege. These two seemingly embedded aspects of Australian social relations are also embedded in the terrain of non-Indigenous/Indigenous race relations. My theoretical framework was the domain of Aboriginality (Walter 2009). As detailed in Chapter 1, this theory operationalizes the power dimensions of non-Indigenous/Indigenous race relations via the continual positioning of Aboriginal and Torres Strait Islander as the "other," socially, politically, culturally, and economically.

Table 4.2: Frequencies of AuSSA questions H1, a through f—Indigenous Attitude Statements

How strongly do you agree or disagree with the following statements?	Agree* %	Neither %	Disagree* %
a. Aboriginal people are now treated equally to other Australians	23	19	58
f. Injustices towards Aboriginal people are now all in the past	26	22	52
c. Aboriginal people should not have to change their culture to fit into Australian society	53	23	25
e. Aboriginal people who no longer follow traditional lifestyles are not really Aboriginal	23	20	58
b. Aboriginal people's levels of disadvantage justifies extra government assistance	45	21	34
d. Granting land rights to Aboriginal people is unfair to other Australians	42	25	33

* Results on Strong Agree and Agree categories and Strongly Disagree and Disagree combined in this table.

Note: The 4 responses from Aboriginal and Torres Strait Islander people were removed from the analysis.

Source: Derived from data from AuSSA 2007

Table 4.3: Frequencies of Non-Indigenous/Indigenous Social Proximity Question

Social Proximity Items	Frequency	Percentage
I mix regularly with Aboriginal people on a day to day basis	245	9
I know Aboriginal people but do not mix regularly with them	1,187	45
I do not know any Aboriginal people personally	1,236	46
Totals	2,668	100

Source: Derived from data from AuSSA 2007

From this topic I posed two research questions (as opposed to survey items) about contemporary race relations. The first was concerned with non-Indigenous attitudes towards Indigenous people and issues, and the second was about the level of social proximity between non-Indigenous people and Indigenous people. Together, the research questions sought to identify the social, demographic, and cultural dimensions of non-Indigenous attitudes towards Indigenous inequality *and* how these related to their actual social interaction with Indigenous people. The first research question was operationalized by a set of survey items that asked respondents how much they agreed/disagreed with six statements about Aboriginal people; two relating to inequality; two relating to culture and identity; and two related to aspects of restorative justice, extra government assistance, and land rights. The aggregated frequency results are included in Table 4.2.

The second research question was operationalized via the inclusion of a non-Indigenous/Indigenous social proximity question. Respondents were asked about their level of interaction with Indigenous people across three levels. The responses were as in Table 4.3.

The analysis of the data from these survey items was conducted over three levels. The univariate frequency counts were followed by a cross-tabulation of the attitude responses with the socio-demographic characteristics of the responders. These results found that in line with other studies (see; Dunn et al. 2004; Goot and Rowse 2007; Goot and Watson 2001; Western 1969) that older, male, less educated, and more rural respondents were significantly more likely to have less egalitarian attitudes towards Aboriginal people and issues. A principle component analysis and reliability analysis also found that the items could be reduced to a single scale. An ordinary least squares multivariate regression, using this scale as the dependent variable, confirmed that, holding all other variables constant, non-Indigenous Australian women, those living in urban areas, those working as professionals, and those with higher education all scored significantly higher Aboriginal attitude scores than non-Indigenous men, those in rural locations, those working in non-professional occupations, and those with less than a bachelor degree education level. The strongest predictor of a high score was being educated to a bachelor degree or above. In the multivariate analysis stage the level of social proximity of the respondents to Aboriginal and Torres Strait Islander people was not significant.

These results were then interpreted through the Domain of Aboriginality theoretical framework. The findings indicate that while a small majority of non-Indigenous Australians recognize the continuation of Indigenous inequality, a significant proportion actively disagree and a similar proportion choose not to agree or disagree. Given the continuation of the readily available dire socio-economic data emerging from the census and other national collections, and the regular media reporting of discrimination, poverty, and poor health outcomes, these results are remarkable. They indicate that Indigenous social inequality has become so normalized within Australian race relations that its pervasive presence is accepted without asking the burning question of how that inequality arises or is sustained.

Similarly, the cultural equality item results are also remarkable. With roughly one quarter of non-Indigenous Australians agreeing that Aboriginal people should have to change their culture to fit in, or lose identity if not traditional, they reflect the dominant position of non-Indigenous Australians within race relations. First, the results demonstrate a basic lack of acceptance of Aboriginal and Torres Strait Islander culture as the original Australian culture—that is, that all "other" cultures are migrant cultures. Second, somewhat inconsistently, there is a refusal to acknowledge that Aboriginal and Torres Strait Islander cultures, like all cultures, cannot be static but must change over time. The culture of the Euro-Australian majority is markedly different from that of the First Fleet arrivals, yet no one suggests that to be truly Euro-Australian one must practice the culture and lifestyles of the first settlers.

Finally, there is the mismatch between the proportions recognizing the continued existence of inequality and injustice and those agreeing to the justice of redress. This finding suggests a dissonance between egalitarian attitudes expressed and a willingness to put those attitudes into action: an attitude/action gap. The interpretation is that the findings reflect the imbalance of power in Australian non-Indigenous/Indigenous relations. Addressing Indigenous rights and structural disadvantage is presumed to lead to a reduction in non-Indigenous privilege. From this conceptual vantage point we can understand why those non-Indigenous Australians with higher education, with their higher status and incomes, are less likely than those from lower socio-economic groups to perceive a risk of loss of privilege, and are therefore more likely to be supportive of remediating strategies.

The finding that less than 10 percent of non-Indigenous Australians mix regularly with Aboriginal people was an illuminating insight into non-Indigenous Australia's relationship with Aboriginal Australia. More enlightening, however, were results showing that interaction or non-interaction with Aboriginal people were not significant factors in their own right in predicting non-Indigenous Australian's Aboriginal issues attitudes. The logical explanation is that these attitudes are formed and held outside of any interaction with real Aboriginal people. The alternative attitudinal framing sources are the dominant discourses of Indigeneity presented within media and political realms. These sources in Australia, to date, are usually pejorative and static. The theoretical conclusion is that the disconnection between interaction *with* Aboriginal people and attitudes *towards* Aboriginal people underpins the non-translation of recognition of continuing inequality into support for remedial actions.

naryi kati Ontology

The ontology that informs *nayri kati* privileges Indigenous world views and Indigenous understandings of who and what we are as peoples and individuals and our place in the world. It incorporates an Indigenous understanding of a world that is defined by our relationships with kin, community, ancestors, country, and place. Perceptions of the lived reality of being colonized Indigenous peoples sequestered within first world nations is reflected in the methodology's focus on non-Indigenous/Indigenous relations (and vice versa). This ontological aspect encompasses how Indigenous people are perceived to "be"—these societies' operational relations with their resident Indigenous peoples. Pragmatically, the ontological frame informing *nayri kati* is also one that challenges *and* exposes the ontological hegemony of Indigenous statistical practice. While statistics do not lie, the version of reality they reflect can, and does, vary. More critically, the statistical story framed through an Indigenous ontological lens will reflect this in both the questions the data seek to answer and the questions the researcher asks of the data.

An Indigenous Ontological Frame

As detailed in Chapter 1, standard Australian quantitative practice promulgates Indigenous data as benign numerical summaries presenting a picture that is objectively real. Not so. The ontological frame is a presumption of pejorative Indigenous racial/cultural difference and a norm of Indigenous deficit. Or more simply, our assertion is that the quantitative research questions asked are shaped by the askers' ontological frame, which extends to the results generated. For example, the central question of the Longitudinal Study of Indigenous Children project discussed earlier is: "How do Australian Indigenous children grow up strong?" (LSIC 2005). This question, developed by a predominantly

Indigenous researcher steering committee, has a specific ontological frame. It seeks information on how our children can grow, develop, and live in a way that maximizes their life chances within and through their Indigeneity. A hypothetical question generated from an ontological frame built around a presumption of pejorative Indigenous racial/cultural difference for a similar longitudinal study of Indigenous children might have asked: "What are the patterns of economic, education and health disadvantage of Australian Indigenous children?" The answers to the former question are to be found in the stories and responses of Indigenous families on data items relating to the capacities and circumstances that operate to best support their raising of strong, healthy, resilient, and happy children in dire socio-economic and culturally marginalizing life circumstances. The answer to the latter question would be an over time examination of Indigenous children, reliant on their continuous comparison against an unquestioned white Australian norm via sets of standard socio-economic and demographic measures. For the first question, the ontological presumption is that the data can portray a unique, compelling picture of contemporary Indigenous peoples within this society, of value and validity in their own right. In the other, the ontological presumption is that the data always need dichotomous comparisons to allow interpretation and to give them substance.

Research Example 3: Mapping the Ontological Landscape

What might seem simple ontological differences lead to significantly different approaches to quantitative research. First, it depends how we understand the reality of our nation. For example, in the Commonwealth of Australia map in Figure 4.3, the light lines indicate the demarcation between the formerly individual colonies, combined under Federation in 1901 to form the six Australian states and two territories. From this perspective I have highlighted the city of Perth and towns of Maningrida and Dubbo as a precursor to the upcoming research example. These state and territory lines of course do not exist in reality. They are a conception of what Australia "is" based on colonization and colonial practices which are given solidity via legal processes. From an Indigenous perspective, Australia "is" very different—Australia is comprised of more than 500 Aboriginal and Torres Strait Islander nations, the boundaries of which may cross contemporary state boundaries. From this perspective I have included in the map, again for the later research example, the nations of the traditional and contemporary owners of the lands on which Perth, Dubbo, and Maningrida sit.

These two perspectives of what is Australia are ontologically different. More crucially, the perspective of the researcher as to which one is the "true" version will likely sharply alter the questions asked and the interpretation of results in any analysis. A project I undertook for the Australian Bureau of Statistics using 2006 Census data offers an insight into this process (see Walter 2008). Writing

Figure 4.3: Australia by Urban Site and Traditional Country

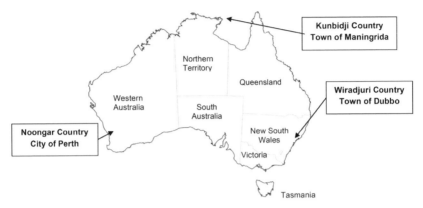

for a predominantly non-Indigenous audience, my first ontological challenge was to disturb the standard practice of aggregating Indigenous data to the national or state level. Rather, I argued, broad stroke labelling under the bland and essentializing category of "the Indigenous population" decontextualizes Indigenous lived experience and blunts the compelling impact of statistical data. Each people has a unique history, affiliation to country, and cultural identity, and their location in specific places and spaces shapes the context and circumstances of their community and individual lives. Three Indigenous nations in their locations were selected for analysis: Kunbidji country at Maningrida, a remote community in the Northern Territory; Wuradjuri country at Dubbo, a regional town in New South Wales; and Noongar country at Perth, the capital city of Western Australia. The distinction between a primarily Indigenous township such as Maningrida with Indigenous/non-Indigenous shared geographic locations of Perth and Dubbo allowed dimensions of spatiality to figure in the interpretative frame alongside the broader social, cultural, political, and economic factors of place.

The second ontological break was to prefix the data analysis with the Indigenous story of each place. The historical and contemporary context was set as the interpretive mechanism for socio-demographic statistics. For example, Dubbo, a regional hub for western New South Wales, is Wiradjuri country and the traditional lands of the Tubbagah people. The Tubbagah people's historical and contemporaneous connection to country is tied to the cultural significance of the Terramungamine area. Systematically dispossessed via frontier violence during the mid 1800s, the remaining people were contained within the Talbaragar Reserve on the outskirts of town where the New South Wales Aboriginal Protection Board regulated every aspect of their lives until the late 1960s. The government closure of the Talbaragar reserve in the 1960s resulted in a heavy concentration of Aboriginal residents within the town's public housing areas.

Now, the public housing "Gordon Estate"—home to a significant proportion of the Tubbagah people—is also being forcibly closed and its mostly Aboriginal residents moved. The history of resistance is also an important context of place. Tubbagah people have never accepted dispossession and oppression. Tubbagah leader William Ferguson launched the Aboriginal Protection Association in 1937 to lobby on behalf of Aboriginal rights and living conditions. In 1995 the Tubbagah people lodged a Native Title Claim over the 16.2 hectare Terramungamine reserve. Although immediately contested by local and state authorities on the basis of public access and the presence of a historic stock trail, an agreement was finally struck in 2002 over protection for Aboriginal burial sites and the preservation of Aboriginal cultural heritage.

The statistical analyses of each place demonstrate a mosaic of similarities and differences between Indigenous lives and across place. Living a Noongar life in Perth differs from living a Tubbagah life in Dubbo or a Kunbidgi life in Maningrida. All three peoples live in the same geographic space as their ancestors, and all have in recent times reasserted, via land claims, the legitimacy of their belonging place. All also share a history of colonization and dispossession from land and subsequent legislative control of their lives. But how these consequences are manifested varies by place. The Kunbidgi people form the majority population in their traditional country at Maningrida. At Dubbo the Tubbagah occupy their traditional space alongside a majority of non-Indigenous residents. And at Perth, the Noongar people form only a tiny minority within a metropolitan population of more than one million.

These locational proximities shape and create different contexts, and the 2006 census data reflect these different lived experiences by place. As shown in Table 4.4, Aboriginal people living in Perth are more likely to own their own home, be educated to Year 12, be in education between the ages of eighteen and twenty-four years of age, and have a higher weekly income than those in Dubbo or Maningrida. In Maningrida, home-ownership, education levels across all spheres, and median income are obviously differently constructed by remoteness, community owned housing stock, and lack of educational facilities and resources. Diversity between places, however, is overwhelmed by the endurance of negative similarities.

As shown in the final column of Table 4.4, compared with non-Indigenous peoples living in the same places (proxied here by national population data), the Indigenous socio-economic position is consistent regardless of geographic location. Across these widely divergent groups, that proportion of the population under the age of fifteen years is double or higher than that of the national (97.5 percent settler) population, while the proportion over the age of sixty-five is less

Table 4.4: Indigenous Figures by Location and National Population Figures

Indicator	Dubbo Indigenous	Perth Indigenous	Maningrida Indigenous	National Population
Aged < 15 years	42.4%	37.4%	36.8%	19.8%
Aged > 65 years	2.9%	2.2%	2.1%	13.%
Median age	17 years	20 years	20 years	37 years
Owner/Purchaser	33.9%	37.6%	6.5%	64.8%
Renter	62.0%	55.5%	90.3%	27.2%
Household with 6+ usual occupants	11.3%	11.5%	92.1%	3.1%
Educated to Year 12	15.6%	21.3%	5.3%	44.9%
Post-school qualifications	12.0%	13.0%	2.6%	44.0%
In education 18–24 years	12.4%	14.6%	na	39.5%
Unemployment rate	21.9%	16.1%	16.4%	5.2%
Labor market participation rate	56.3%	51.1%	44.7%	64.6%
Median weekly individual income	$306	$327	$209	$466

Source: Derived from Australian Census Data 2006

than a quarter that of the total population. In the urban areas of Perth and Dubbo home ownership rates are only a little over half of the national level, and rates of overcrowding four times as high. Unemployment rates are at least three times the national level despite lower levels of labor force participation and rates of post school qualifications, and grade 12 achievement less than a third of national levels. That the proportion of Aboriginal youth in education aged eighteen to twenty-four in the urban areas is less than a third of that of their settler compatriots indicates that this depressing picture is not likely to change in the short term.

The statistical picture that emerges from this analysis is that although 75 percent of Aboriginal and Torres Strait Islander people live in the same geographic places as non-Indigenous Australians, we reside in different demographic and socio-economic realms. This analysis also provides compelling evidence to support a reversing of the ontological lens from "What are the socio-demographic differences between Indigenous and non-Indigenous people?" to "Why do these differences exist?" The Aboriginal populations of these places are from very different Aboriginal nations historically, culturally, and in regard to the social and geographical circumstances under which they currently live their lives. Yet their socio-economic positioning in relation to the socio-economic positioning of their respective settler populations is remarkably similar. Through a domain of Aboriginality theoretical framework, the question might equally be asked: "Why do Australian settler populations always occupy a position of dramatic socio-economic privilege in relation to Aboriginal populations, regardless of location?" Such an ontological lens compels very different research questions that differ greatly from the current dominant Australian research agenda.

Conclusion

We hope that this demonstration of Indigenous quantitative methodology in practice via the example of *nayri kati* demonstrates how quantitative methods can be successfully integrated and form an integral aspect of a valid Indigenous methodology. Indigenous quantitative methodologies can and do provide radically different statistical insights into Indigenous peoples. As critically, Indigenous quantitative methodologies can, and do, provide insights into white settler colonizing peoples and institutions, especially in their relationship to first world Indigenous peoples. In the following chapter, we explore similar issues in a Canadian context.

Notes

1 Capitalization of proper nouns is not a feature of the Tasmanian language palawa kani.

2 As *nayri kati* is a methodology used by author Walter, the singular voice is used in this part of the chapter.

3 Trucanini was survived for several years by Tasmanian women kidnapped by sealers to the Kangaroo Island off South Australia.

4 The description of the Domain of Aboriginality is summarized but also builds on parts of an earlier article: Walter 2009, "An Economy of Poverty: Power and the Domain of Aboriginality."

5 I have overheard similar casual denigrating conversations about Native American and Canadian Aboriginal peoples while visiting those countries.

Chapter 5

Indigenous Quantitative Methodological Practice— Canada

Introduction

This chapter details a quantitative Indigenous research methodology wedded to Hokowhitu's (2009) theory of Indigenous density or "immediacy" (detailed in Chapter 1) to explain how dominant quantitative methodologies can be reconfigured for Indigenous community benefit. In this context, the chapter's second part explores the Canadian census's inability to enumerate Aboriginal sociality, in three contexts: a tribally specific context, an urban context, and a Métis national context. These are important issues insofar as both represent forms of Indigeneity every bit as legitimate as others currently in place and, likewise, they both speak to central tenets of my own Indigeneity.[1] The major difference between them is that they largely fail to conform to the needs of existing official policy requirements. In emphasizing these three case studies, I seek to denaturalize the context within which official statistics are constructed and, thus, offer a basis for their *de*construction and alternative possibilities.

I should begin by saying that my critique of the information currently being produced is not being launched at the technical level. These categories produce legitimate statistical information within their conceptual boundaries. My point is simply—but importantly—that other categories can produce alternative and *equally legitimate* statistical information. In other words, the methodology, rather than the method, is problematic. I thus take two points from Bruce Curtis's (2001: 35) critical stance toward census-making to assist us in thinking about alternatives. First, censuses should possess a high level of "inter-subjective agreement" between enumerator and enumeratee: "The criteria adopted for evaluating census making should be found in the character

Indigenous Statistics: A Quantitative Research Methodology by Maggie Walter and Chris Andersen, 111–129. © 2013 Left Coast Press, Inc. All rights reserved.

of the social relations themselves"; and second, since not all statistical configurations of social relations are created equal, different configurations offer "different practical possibilities for intervention and administration," and as such, "the worth of census data [and quantitative research more generally] is related to the projects in whose service they are enlisted."

In this chapter I explore a different configuration of Indigenous sociality in light of the important considerations that Curtis (2001) details. One increasingly important element of contemporary Canadian Indigenous sociality that sits largely outside the ability of current statistical configurations to document is the emerging urban Indigenous communities that have emerged as engines of cultural Indigenous power in both Australia and Canada. While official quantitative data analysts have begun to explore these social relations, they do so by cross tabulating existing census classifications with geographical residence. The chapter's third and final part will explain the problems with attempting to "pour new wine into old bottles," and how we might go about creating a new set of analytical lenses better suited for dealing with the Indigenous sociality of these novel and distinctive communities.

Example 1: Tribal Affiliations as Ethnic Ancestry

I have written elsewhere about the ways in which Statistics Canada measures ethnic ancestry and the problems this presents for enumerating changes between Aboriginal categories—what Statistics Canada officials refer to as "ethnic drift" or "ethnic mobility" (Andersen 2013b). As explained in various parts of this book, current census categories are employed not because they measure Indigenous "identity" better or more accurately than other alternative categories might, but because they better measure the *kinds* of knowledge required as evidence for deficit-based policy interventions. But, as this chapter outlines, there is nothing acontextually superior about such categories and, indeed, the positioning of these as measuring "identity" to the exclusion of other, equally contextual measures naturalizes particular ways of understanding Indigenous peoples, our communities, and the issues within them.

Back to the issue of ethnic ancestry. We explained in Chapter 1 how notions of "ethnic ancestry" have been embedded into development-based discourses. Here, I want to describe a different way to enumerate Indigenous identity—through tribal identity. I am not suggesting that tribal identity and "ethnic" identity are identical (to do so is to efface the realities of Indigenous sovereignty that separate them). Nonetheless, thinking in terms of official identification, tribal identities offer a particular *kind* of collective identification, despite the fact that contemporary policy makers seem to hold little interest in these forms of affiliation.

In the previous chapter, Walter explored the ways in which changing the ontological landscape within which we understand Indigeneity—from the conventional mapping of Australia to one focused more specifically on Indigenous national boundaries—changes the ways in which we understand and enumerate it. The same is true, though in a different way, in Canada. As it stands, Statistics Canada officially enumerates Aboriginality according to two major questions, with several additional sub-questions depending on the answers provided to the first two. To provide some contextualization, we will detail some of the history behind why the current categories exist as they do and their relationship to Canada's colonial history.

Canada's Constitution recognizes three distinct Aboriginal peoples— First Nations (formerly termed "Indians"); Inuit (formerly termed "Eskimos"); and Métis (formerly termed "Half-breeds" and "Metis"), but these are administrative distinctions that relate to the Canadian government's attempts to govern the diversity of Indigenous peoples in Canada, rather than reflecting "real" or exhaustive accountings of Indigenous identities. For example, the term 'First Nations' encapsulates dozens of distinctive tribal societies that, while sharing broad cosmological similarities, nonetheless exhibit massive differences in their internal and external governance of language, lifestyle, land tenure, and gender relations, to name but a few of many sectors of social life. To provide one of many examples: Canada's "Indigenous population" possesses more than fifty languages from a dozen different language groups.

Despite this distinctiveness and diversity, British, and later Canadian, governing rationalities and policy was never intended to reflect this diversity. Instead, the major category through which they understood Indigenous peoples and attempted to produce governing policy was that of "Indian," and before that, "friend and foe" (Tobias 1991), based in pre-confederate social and political dynamics of imperialism (Day 2000; Dickason 1992; Tobias 1991). Early relations were largely based in European sovereignty-based concerns with marking and claiming territory (see Hogeveen 1999).

In the Indigenous territories that eventually came to be claimed by Canada, these concerns first assumed the guise of England and the Hudson's Bay Company, through the former granting the Royal Charter of 1670 to the latter, and the relations of domination and subservience particular to the fur trade relations that followed in its wake. Concomitant with this rationality of accumulation, Indigenous territories were also variously claimed (often without their knowledge) in a larger game of imperial power between England and France, and later the United States. Following the Seven Years War in the mid eighteenth century and the subsequent creation of treaties and agreements of friendship and collaboration, imperial claims to Indigenous territories began to stabilize. Despite this early if grudging equality, Aboriginal settlements and nations in "Canadian" territory came increasingly under the ambit of British imperial control.

Early relations between Aboriginal nations and various imperial powers were characterized by an uneasy equality, likely fueled by mutual trade concerns. While this uneasy and often fragile equality shaped the protective stance of initial attempts at formal policy through which the British government attempted to ward off the growing intrusion of non-Indigenous settlers (exemplified in the precepts of the *Royal Proclamation of 1763*), governing rationalities from the non-Indigenous side remained powerfully anchored in the rule of difference alluded to in the Introduction (Chatterjee 1993) as the central marker of global colonial rule. By the end of the inter-empire rivalries with France and the United States at the dawn of the nineteenth century, Aboriginal communities suddenly found themselves targeted as "impediments to progress" and in need of "civilization," rather than as the "valued allies" of their earlier relationships. Initial official attempts to "civilize" targeted Indigenous individuals' moral capacity through their "souls" in the form of religious instruction and (in some cases) physical removal from the corrupting influences of white society. By the era of Canadian confederation in 1867, however, these interventions had turned into more deliberate and calculated attempts at assimilation.

During and following the treaty era (roughly the period between 1870 and 1920), Aboriginal communities—most extremely status Indian communities (described in Chapter 1)—came under increasing surveillance from Canadian government authorities, including the then-termed Department of Indian Affairs, the North West Mounted Police (a national policing agency formed in the 1870s), and the church. Interventionist techniques began to include the rationing of food, the imposition of a pass system controlling movement on- and off-reserve for those designated as "Indians," the outlawing of ceremonies (though these interventions were uneven in their application), the imposition of Christianity, an expectation to take up farming, and the large-scaled creation of "residential schools" (for general overviews, see Dickason 1992; Miller 1989; Ray 2008). Such measures were widely viewed by contemporaneous authorities as a midway point in the eventual assimilation of the "Indian problem" and the disappearance of Indians.

Importantly, the rationalities undergirding this intervention were shot through with Victorian racializing and patriarchal mentalities, particularly (though not only) for those classified as "Indians." Indeed, legislation such as the 1876 *Indian Act* and the racism and patriarchy woven into its rules and regulations not only served as the basis for intervention into "Indian" communities, it shaped the very boundaries of the communities themselves. Once adopted as common practices of administrative policy, these policies enacted horrendous impacts on the kin relations of Indigenous women in particular, as well as their children.

Nonetheless, the term 'Indian' became—and remains—the mainstay through which the complexity of Indigenous society was rendered visible to

Canada's government, and a bulk of its knowledge about Indigenous peoples has keyed off this one term. Particularly, through the Department of Indian Affairs, Canada's "Indian policy" enacted horrendous policies on tens of thousands of Aboriginal people in hundreds of Aboriginal communities across the country. Given the Department of Indian Affairs's detailed colonial knowledge about Native communities, it is little wonder that the history of census-taking and the categories of its enumeration have been so deeply rooted in the colonial rationalities animating Indian Affairs administration. This included both biological understandings of race (and racial "mixedness") and an associated patriarchy through which "Indian" was defined legislatively and through which the Department of Indian Affairs excluded (formerly) status Indian women and their families upon their marriage to non-status men (see Eberts 2010; Palmater 2011).

From its 1871 inception in the census, the category "Indian" was, of course, derived from Department of Indian Affairs legislation. Likewise, through most of the twentieth century, census enumerator instructions for collecting Aboriginal "ethnic ancestry" information required ascertaining the patrilineage of "Indian" respondents (that is, ascertaining whether the respondent's father was "Indian") rather than, for example, tribal affiliation. Not uncoincidentally, this fit squarely into policy requirements of the *Indian Act*. From the standpoint of longer standing ethnic ancestry like that found in tribal affiliation and broader kinship dynamics, however, such classifications wreaked havoc (see Lawrence 2004; Simpson 2008). Despite the numerous changes to the official meaning and boundaries of legal "Indianness" the category itself has displayed a remarkable endurance. Buoyed by a now-massive infrastructure geared toward the integration of "Indians" into the mainstream Canadian body politic, the term's legitimacy enfolded its census visage to sit at the largely unquestioned center of Canada's colonial/administrative "Aboriginal policy."

Despite their widespread use and longstanding legitimacy, however, the current census categories are not the only logical categories that could be used to produce knowledge about the Aboriginal population in Canada. Arguably, equally (if not more so) contextual indicators of identity can theoretically be derived from existing ethnic ancestry data produced in the existing "long-form" National Household Survey. For example, question 17 of the current National Household Survey asks, "What were the ethnic or cultural origins of this person's ancestors?" with the caveat that the term "ancestor" refers to someone more distant than a grandparent (Statistics Canada 2011: 10). Among the twenty-eight options listed as examples of ancestral ethnic cultures, the form includes "Cree, Mi'kmaq, Salish, Métis, Inuit" as Aboriginal examples.

Two problems prevent any data analysis and (thus) knowledge production using a tribal context. First, Statistics Canada does not publicly release data pertaining to tribal affiliation. As such, even if tribal policy makers (or any policy makers, for that matter) wished to apply for grants using publicly available, tribally specific data, they couldn't. A second sub-question of the Aboriginal identity question allows respondents to fill in their "First Nation" and so might serve as a (imperfect) proxy, not everyone fills these out and not all First Nations are included. But even in this case, the aspiring statistician would likely have to contact Statistics Canada directly (or, given current privacy legislation, become employed with them) in order to get access to this information. Likewise, while Aboriginal "first language" could also be used as a proxy for tribal affiliation, we run into the same problems in terms of how the census question is posed (in terms of language competency[2]).

In addition to the problem of not releasing the data publicly, it is unlikely that even if it were available, policy makers—Aboriginal or non- —would find it useful. This is because in Canada the current categories of analysis are so powerfully entrenched in the Aboriginal policy field (for reasons explained in Chapter 1) that any data produced in a tribal context would be of little value to the kinds of grants applied for and auditing requirements levied by various funding organizations. This is particularly problematic in an urban context where much of the funding supporting Indigenous social services organizations in Canadian cities is short term/year-to-year funding with onerous grant-writing requirements and, more often than not, "status free" requirements, meaning that the service organization must admit Aboriginal clientele regardless of their legal categorization (see Andersen and Strachan 2012).

And yet. Given the internal diversity of Indigenous societies and given the broad span of colonial projects across such a geographically expansive landscape, we should not be surprised that Indigenous peoples encountered, endured, and reacted to colonial projects differently, for a wide variety of reasons relating to location, governing structures, and the eras within which colonial authorities attempted to colonize them. Likewise, the same diversity could reasonably be expected of the kinds of social conditions they find themselves and their communities in today. There are a number of reasons, then, to think that tribally specific data might be useful in ways that the current data categories are not.

Another level at which we can think about this is to recall Curtis's (2001: 35) observation about the worth of census data: different configurations offer "different practical possibilities for intervention and administration" and, as such, "the worth of census data [and quantitative research more generally] is related to the projects in whose service they are enlisted." In Canada, the Assembly of First Nations is the national organization that purports to speak on behalf of the vast bulk of all First Nations in Canada. Part of the organization's problem, however, has always been that of dealing with the diversity of First Nations within it. One way tribally specific data might be useful would be in the context of making tribally specific claims within the organization itself.

It might prove equally useful, however, in the context of building links around language regeneration, tribally specific tribal justice courts, youth culture camps, health programming, or any number of projects that would benefit from tribally specific data. In particular, taking seriously the assumption about the importance of "culturally specific" programming, best practice information might prove useful according to tribally specific data. As we will explore further in the second case study, Canada has created a number of Aboriginal peoples "post-censal" surveys to produce more specific information on several sectors of social life (health and children's health in particular), and in doing so, has asked literally hundreds of questions that would, if cross-listed with tribally specific responses, prove invaluable to the projects just listed, not to mention numerous others. We turn to that discussion now.

Example 2: Urban Aboriginal Communities (Not) in the Census

Over the past four decades, the Canadian federal government has begun to pay increased policy attention to the urban Aboriginal communities that have formed in many of its cities. Australia's Aboriginal population is proportionately more urbanized than Canada's,[3] but the two countries nonetheless share a surprising number of structural similarities in both the processes of urbanization and in their current configurations. So, while this chapter's argument is presented in a Canadian context, it resonates in other Indigenous first world contexts as well. More broadly, while Indigeneity is often authenticated in rough relation to its connection to land, rural spaces, and their attendant spirituality, urban Indigeneity has proven itself an engine of Indigenous cultural power, producing novel and distinctive sets of social relations that, while rooted in previous relations, are not limited to or by them (see Peters and Andersen 2013 for a broad discussion of urban Indigeneity in an international context). This newness and its separation from many of the policy silos previously used to govern Indigenous communities limit the ability of current statistical categories to explore urban Indigeneity's empirical nuances.

Traditionally, official statistics used to document urban Aboriginal communities in Canada are derived from a simple cross-tabulation of the various socio-demographical indicators deemed relevant with geographical residence. In Canada, this has produced estimates demonstrating in broad strokes that this population comprises slightly more than half of all Aboriginal people in Canada and that we are demographically better off—in some cases, far better off—than those living in rural locales. From a policy perspective largely rooted in developmental rationalities focused on "narrowing the gap," it would therefore appear that urban Indigenous communities are in less need of official policy attention than more rurally based ones. Indeed, in terms of Canadian monies spent on the "Native problem," the budget for dealing with urban Aboriginal issues is disproportionately small in comparison. Still, in comparison to their *non-*Aboriginal counterparts, the urban Aboriginal population is younger and more mobile (that is, we tend to move more often) with lower rates of post-secondary education.[4] In other words, the population's demographic characteristics continue to exhibit characteristics of interest to Aboriginal policy makers.

Like the data used more generally for Aboriginal population statistics, the urban Aboriginal population is documented using "identity" population estimates. As discussed in Chapter 3, however, we might ask what makes it an urban Indigenous "identity" population when the categories used to "create" it were themselves fashioned in the context of historically rural policy concerns (and populations) that bear little in common with the "livedness" of urban social relations? Urban Aboriginal communities are distinct and growing: the configurations of social power that mark them are specific in ways that make it unlikely to be understood through categories created in the context of on-reserve colonial administrative policies now more than a century old. Existing statistical categories and definitions only *seem* effective or accurate because they have been understood and positioned for so long as objective and neutral, corresponding to some underlying reality.

We may nonetheless understand census categories (per Curtis's [2001] discussion) as being rooted in particular assumptions about the social relations being examined and intervened upon. In this alternative context, we can see in a very practical way how, although they conjure up only partial elements of a fuller complexity, existing statistical configurations nonetheless continue to be positioned as impartial, objective, and widespread accounts of those relations. Sure, most statisticians would likely not argue that cross-tabulating geographical residency with various socio-demographic indicators captures the full complexity. But then, there is no need to: these configurations represent virtually the only evidence available upon which policy can be based and, as such, are acted on by policy actors regardless of their partiality.

At one level, claiming a distinctiveness to urban Aboriginal identities should be fairly uncontroversial. Much of the recent theorizing on identity positions it as socially constructed, and, therefore, the immediate contexts within which identity is produced should shape it in a manner distinctive from other contexts. Indeed, it might not only seem uncontroversial but obvious to expect urban contexts to produce distinctly urban Aboriginal identities (see Andersen 2013a). In Canada, however, federal policy has long been based on the notion that as certain administrative categories of Aboriginals became urbanized (or perhaps more precisely, moved to urban areas), the federal government was no longer responsible for them, and therefore, no policies for dealing with urban contexts were necessary (see Andersen and Strachan 2012; Graham and Peters 2002). Hence, federal policy in Canada has largely—and until recently, intergenerationally—failed to recognize anything distinctive about urban Aboriginality deserving specific policy attention.

What happens, however, if we begin with a starting point, one that presupposes the distinctiveness, and indeed the analytical separateness of, urban Aboriginal identities (and policy-relevant policy categories!) from currently existing Aboriginal categories like "Indian," "Métis," and "Inuit" (with their various sub-categorizations)? Given that estimates for the so-called identity population are generated in light of the three principle categories just listed, we can reasonably take away from them the idea that Statistics Canada does not find individual Indigenous self-identification in itself useful for governance but, rather, only as it fits into relevant administrative categories. In an urban context where such categories are playing catch up with a set of social relations still emerging and not yet congealed in the manner of rural social relations like those of First Nations, there is nothing irresponsible about asking fundamental questions about what we might ask *instead*.

In a recent edited collection (Andersen 2013a), I detailed a number of elements comprising the distinctiveness of urban Indigenous communities. Several of these are easily discernable from existing statistical configurations and census categories, but importantly, many are not, nor are they collectively easily configured in ways that match existing policy priorities. Moreover, we are not suggesting that any one of the elements in its isolation supports the argument for the distinctiveness of urban Aboriginal communities, nor are we suggesting that rural communities (like First Nations in Canada) are not individually distinctive in their own right. Taken together, however—and accounting for some of the local vernacularity sure to accompany them—they mark urban Indigenous life in ways that qualitatively (and quantitatively!) differ from non-urban communities.

The various elements of urban Aboriginal communities included: 1) Aboriginal economic marginalization that takes place largely in the context of non-Aboriginal prosperity; 2) a growing professional/middle class that is beginning to produce a class division in urban Aboriginal communities; 3) the particular character of racism/social exclusion that involves daily interactions with non-Aboriginal residents; 4) the Indigenous diversity within the community, including cultural, linguistic, legal, and intergenerational; 5) urban Aboriginal institutions relating to social service delivery and beyond that must deal with the distinctive diversity discussed in point four; 6) the distinctive character of urban Aboriginal policy as it relates to the lack of a federally led "universal" policy for dealing with urban Aboriginal issues; and 7) the character of informal networks that continue to include extended kin but also relationships with other Aboriginal residences of different tribes, cultures, and linguistic communities.

In addition to these elements, others include: 8) a continued attachment to non-urban communities in a manner for which the reverse is not true; 9) struggles over political representation, especially as urban Aboriginal organizations begin to claim responsibility for individuals whose "home" communities also claim responsibility; 10) the place(s) of Aboriginal women in urban contexts, in terms of both the increased likelihood of their formal public power *and* their victimization in various sex trades; and finally—and perhaps most important to understanding the Canadian context—11) the city-city distinctive character of urban Aboriginality. While this list is certainly not exhaustive and these choices can be debated, we believe nonetheless that they sketch out the broad contours of a distinctive set of urban Indigenous social relations and, therefore, a distinctive urban Indigenous identity[5] (see Andersen 2013a for a lengthier discussion of these elements).

How would we construct a new statistical configuration attentive to the distinctive elements of urban Aboriginal identities just discussed, and what would it look like? Perhaps conveniently, we believe it neither responsible nor useful to deductively set out a new statistical configuration without broad consultation with the urban Aboriginal communities themselves. Certainly, and despite our criticisms of the existing census configurations, many members of urban Indigenous communities might choose to continue with them (a "pick the devil you know" arrangement). Indeed, those heavily involved in social service delivery are often just as deeply invested in these categories as "authoritative communities" (Curtis 2001) like government agencies (in ways that impact the very constitution of those communities[6]). Conversely, however, other urban Indigenous communities might find such configurations constraining to the goals and objectives specific to their urban locales.

It is perhaps important to note that existing census instruments can deal with some of this complexity in a manner that summary "identity population" estimates like those derived from the National Household Survey cannot. For example, in 1991 Census Canada created a post-censal survey called the *Aboriginal Peoples Survey* (APS). Due to political wrangling with several Aboriginal political organizations, the survey eventually measured various socio-demographic characteristics of the off-reserve Aboriginal population only. The most recent cycle of the APS—nearly two hundred pages in length— asks literally hundreds of in-depth questions relating to issues like household composition, marriage status, residential mobility, educational attainment, Aboriginal language use and fluency, residential school attendance, labor market activities and current status, engagement in traditional activities, sources of personal income, pregnancy and childbirth, height and weight, general health, chronic health conditions, injuries, mental health, distress, thoughts of suicide, smoking alcohol and drug use activities, food security, feelings of community support, and, finally, housing (see APS 2012).

Given that the APS's sample (drawn from the original census) only applies to off-reserve respondents (the majority of whom are urban-based), APS would seem to allow for greater analyses of urban Aboriginal community characteristics. However, the APS suffers from the same issue as the National Household Survey (NHS) , which only interviews a subsample of respondents who self-identified according to one of the NHS's administrative categories. The APS question is, "Are you an Aboriginal person, that is, First Nations, Métis or Inuk (Inuit)? First Nations includes Status and Non-Status Indians" (APS 2012: 5 of 179). Any respondents who indicated Aboriginal ethnic ancestry without self-identifying according to policy categories were excluded from the survey. The reason for this, as indicated earlier, is simple and easily defensible: "The information collected will be used by Aboriginal organizations, groups and communities as well as government to help plan programs and policies in such areas as education, employment and health."[7] Hence, the socio-demographic characteristics of those indicating ancestry without policy-relevant self-identification are deemed of little value and, as such, do not figure in the current configuration of Aboriginal policy-making in Canada. That does not mean, however, that important information could not be collected over a wider spectrum of Aboriginality were policy makers to take a policy interest in the non-policy identity Aboriginal ethnic ancestry population as well.

Stepping back to look at this picture more broadly, it appears that what is required is neither a discussion of possible new categories nor a better process for deciding on what these configurations would look like. For example, Statistics Canada is justifiably proud of their current consultation process: in explaining the design process of the APS, they explain that the design process "brought together expertise from a diverse group of researchers and subject matter experts from within and outside of Statistics Canada."[8] Moreover, since Canada's Aboriginal policy environment necessarily takes place under the auspices of its largest government ministries (in this case predominantly Aboriginal Affairs and Northern Development Canada, Health Canada, and Human Resources and Skills Development Canada), the categories from which statistical information is derived will reflect each government ministry's policy concerns. The same is true for those who derive their grants from these policies and who interact with clientele based broadly upon these categories.

Instead, perhaps, what is required is a commitment to what Ryan Walker (2008) has termed "transformative planning," in which key urban policy makers at all government levels ensure broad collaboration with urban Aboriginal communities and their members. This would not only go a long way toward ensuring more respectful policy relations, it would also increase the likelihood of statistical imaginaries that transcend existing lenses for examining the Aboriginal policy world. It may well be that urban Aboriginal communities in fact decide to "pick the devil they know" and continue to use existing census categories tethered to policy-identity priorities. In such instances, it may well come to pass that existing census classifications—especially those contained in the deeply detailed Aboriginal People Survey—may suffice for their policy information needs (see Andersen 2013b for a broader discussion of these issues).

It may well be, though, that urban Aboriginal communities instead decide to build a more complex and endogamous set of categories through which they think about themselves collectively. In such cases, existing census information will be of little use and, in fact, might even be counterproductive to the policy goals and priorities of the community. For example, in 1997 the (then) Office of the Federal Interlocutor for Métis and Non-Status Indians (OFI[9]) inaugurated an Urban Aboriginal Strategy (UAS) as a means of improving the social and economic opportunities of urban Aboriginals in Canada in a number of cities with substantial Aboriginal populations. In partnership with various urban Aboriginal policy actors, its terms and conditions focused on the improvement of life skills and job and entrepreneurial skills, with a specific emphasis on supporting Aboriginal women, children, and families (Urban Aboriginal Strategy 2005) and with an eye toward building self-reliance and increasing life choices for urban Aboriginals. In this context, UAS hoped to increase the efficiency and coordination of the *existing* urban Aboriginal policy landscape.

Each of the thirteen Canadian cities tagged by UAS was charged with fashioning a model of coordination and engagement. In Edmonton, Alberta,[10] this charge manifested itself in *Wicihitowin: Circle of Shared Responsibility & Stewardship*. As part of the process of creating Wicihitowin, local urban Aboriginal community members engaged in a three-year consultation process that included both quantitative and qualitative components. Through this community-led process, the predecessor to Wicihitowin identified three priorities: identifying urgent issues and priorities; creating an Accord Relationship Agreement to provide a set of principles and values so as to establish working relations; and creating a community mechanism for New Ways of Working together, now called "Wicihitowin: Circle of Shared Responsibility and Stewardship" (2012).[11] In this context Wicihitowin eventually created a number of "community- and action-circles" dedicated to various priorities. Four action circles prioritized Aboriginal youth, men, women, and elders. The action circles prioritized economic development, employment and training, justice, arts and culture, health and well-being, a "welcome to the city" circle, education, housing, and a research circle to assist in providing information for the other action circles.[12]

What is most interesting about this process from a policy perspective is the three years of community consultation—titled "Your City, Your Voice"—that preceded the eventual creation of Wicihitowin. From July to December 2005, this community dialogue process interacted with more than 1,800 local Aboriginal residents. The resulting summary report explains that

> throughout the process, the Elders Circle provided guidance to not only ensure that proper cultural and spiritual protocols were followed, but also to provide needed insights into urban Aboriginal cultures. To this end, a variety of Indigenous methods were used to facilitate the listening and the building of relations in a good way. These included culturally appropriate Open Houses, Talking Circles, Executive Forum and the "Your City, Your Voice" workbook surveys. (Edmonton Urban Aboriginal Dialogue 2006: 10)

From our perspective, the inclusion of the workbook surveys as part of the "Indigenous methods" is a positive step. A thousand of these workbooks were distributed, and roughly 50 percent were completed. Unlike dominant government-led questionnaires, the Wicihitowin "workbooks" asked respondents about their ancestry rather than how they self-identified (though they offered the same categories as the census uses to capture self-identification).

The workbooks were meant to capture five aspects deemed policy-important to the urban Aboriginal community of Edmonton: 1) the extent to which Edmonton is a welcoming city for Aboriginal peoples; 2) issues affecting urban Aboriginal people in Edmonton; 3) new ways of working together; 4) the value of a relationship agreement between the City of Edmonton and urban Aboriginal people in Edmonton—an "Accord"; and 5) guiding principles for a relationship agreement.[13] The important point here for us is that (assuming its methodological validity, which we cannot speak to) the data produced through this process in effect created an almost entirely alternative—yet equally legitimate—set of statistical summaries for the urban Aboriginal community of Edmonton. Moreover, it was far more cognizant of the on-the-ground needs and priorities of that community (in a phrase, it operated according to an Indigeneity of immediacy) than could ever hope to be deduced through existing census classifications.

Example 3: National Métis Statistics

In Example 1, I provided a fairly in-depth administrative history of Britain's, and later Canada's, attempts to govern Indigenous communities. However, this history was skewed heavily toward a discussion about "Indians" or First Nations. This is defensible on a number of grounds, not the least of which is that First Nations comprise the largest administrative bloc of Aboriginals in Canada, have endured the most intensive relationship with the federal government, and have demonstrated the highest level of diversity with respect to languages, lifestyles, and geographical locations. Nonetheless, other Indigenous peoples endured

Canada's attempts to govern them in ways distinctively different from those that impacted First Nations communities. I am referring to the Métis people.

The Métis are an Indigenous people whose origins can be found in the growth of the so-called "buffalo robe" trade on the nineteenth century northern plains (see Peterson 2012; St-Onge et al. 2012). Part of a broad and polyethnic fur trade society that had emerged and stabilized in the nineteenth century, the Métis shared many characteristics with other "post-contact" Indigenous peoples (see St-Onge 2009). Rising to economic prominence by the middle of the nineteenth century and centered in and around Red River (what is now Winnipeg, Manitoba, a province in western Canada), Métis buffalo hunters and fur traders more generally competed with non-Indigenous fur traders for their share of the massive buffalo herds that roamed the northern plains (Ens 1996).

Two little known events in the latter part of the nineteenth century powerfully shaped how the Canadian state came to govern the Métis in ways distinctive from their governing strategies for First Nations. In 1869, the Hudson's Bay Company, granted the land by an English prince in the seventeenth century, "sold" to a newly confederated Canada the territories that Métis and First Nations claimed as their own. In 1870, Canada sent in officials to survey "their" newly acquired territory, and their official cartographies clashed with those used by the Métis who lived part of their year in the region. The Métis famously rebuffed those attempts, several battles ensued, and the Métis formed a provisional government as the traditional owners of the territory that Canada came to claim (see Stanley 1992 [1960]; Tough 1992). In 1870, the prime minister of Canada (Sir John A. MacDonald) negotiated an agreement with the Métis to provide 1.4 million acres of land.

In the years following this negotiated agreement, the Canadian government lagged in its duties to fulfill its land obligations. Meanwhile, the land was flooded with non-Métis immigrants. Many Métis left during these early years, moving to different parts of Canada and the northern United States, often to settle with kin who already lived there. By the 1880s, the dishonorable actions of the Canadian government had morphed from grumbling and grievances into an armed uprising by the Métis. This led to further battles, but in the end, the Métis people's political power was destroyed at the hands of Canada's militia.

With the loss of their power, Métis individuals and communities were shoehorned into a state taxonomy created to deal with First Nations rather than the Métis. Métis in Canada are often seen as "mixed ancestry" in a way other Indigenous peoples are not. From a census standpoint, as the Canadian government began to collect information on Indigenous communities and individuals, they made use of a single "Indian" category. Since no room was made for Métis, from the 1870s onward Métis were denied an empirical census presence. Indeed, with one exception in 1941, Census category had no ability to enumerate Métis specifically until 1991, when the category "Métis" was added to the post-censal Aboriginal Peoples Survey.

As it currently stands in the NHS, only two questions elicit information on Métis enumeratees. The alert reader might have guessed that these relate to the same questions discussed in Chapter 1—ethnic ancestry and identity. Recall that question 17 of the NHS asks: "What were the ethnic or cultural origins of this person's ancestors?" From an "identity" standpoint, question 18 asks, "Is this person an Aboriginal person, that is, First Nations (North American Indian), Métis or Inuk (Inuit)?" Among the response categories is "Yes, Métis." This answer category might appear obvious from an administrative standpoint, but from a Métis national standpoint it eviscerates any possibility of producing an empirically reliable estimate of the number of Métis. Why is this the case?

To elaborate on the point I made above about Métis being understood as "mixed," this mixedness competes with nationhood as the two major conceptual categories available to most Canadians for thinking about Métis identity. In the introduction we used Bourdieu's notion of habitus and investment to think about the ways we come to order our social worlds—that is, how we come to see them as settled or natural. For those who feel an allegiance to the Métis nation (described earlier), the census question allows them an easy opportunity to establish that allegiance empirically. From this perspective, you might think it fairly straightforward to use census data to produce empirical depictions of this nation, in a manner similar to, for example, Quebec, which though formally a province, understands itself as a distinct "nation within a nation."

However, the racialization that undergirds colonial projects (defined in endnote 2) and the extensive intermixing that has occurred through past centuries among *all* Indigenous and non-Indigenous peoples means that because Indigenous self understanding includes an emphasis on their mixed Indigenous and non-Indigenous ancestry, many Indigenous individuals come to self-identify as Métis. This is so, even when they possess no allegiance to the Métis people and no Métis ancestors (see Andersen 2011). And, because the Canadian federal government is loathe to recognize Indigenous communities as "Indians" (many of whose ancestors were cut out of the Indian Act), with a couple of notable exceptions, there is nothing to be gained by making an argument for self understanding as First Nation in whatever tribal variant might be possible.

Why is this an issue with specific respect to the census question in the 2011 NHS? Simply put, because the census's question can't distinguish between these self-understandings of Métis. That is, when those filling off the census check off "Métis," census officials have no idea what they mean when they do so. For many census demographers—especially those who work at Statistics Canada—this isn't necessarily a problem, since most of them have equally internalized racialized notions of Métis identity. Having said that, Statistics Canada authors who publish the data in the different formats they use to disseminate it publicly are quick to acknowledge the validity of the Métis nation. I have written about this elsewhere (see Andersen 2008, forthcoming) and have no wish to repeat myself here except to say that, generally speaking, increases in the Métis population are pinned on two interrelated processes: increased pride in being Métis due to various social events of the last two decades (including court cases Métis have won) and, from there, an increased likelihood of people identifying as Métis who would not have done so in the past (see Andersen 2013b).

The problem is that even when acknowledging these changes, Statistics Canada's interpretation is followed with an empirical description of data derived from categories that capture more than the "ethnic" mobility described in the preceding paragraph (see Andersen 2013b). Moreover, while the public who make use of the data might also agree with these summaries, the data they receive fails to differentiate between two competing uses of the term. This is because Statistics Canada violently slams together what are in fact two opposing self-understandings of Métis, as though the ensuing data spoke to an underlying unity. In a sense, once the decision is made that these data are valuable and once they are released to the public, it can be no other way.

It is thus a small step to take this deep internal cleft within the category itself and turn it into a confident articulation that "nearly nine of 10 Métis live in the western provinces and Ontario" (Statistics Canada 2008: 31); that "seven out of 10 Métis lived in urban areas" (2008: 31); that "Winnipeg is home to the largest number of urban Métis" (2008: 32); the "Métis population still young but has aged" (2008: 33); "Métis children twice as likely to live with a lone parent" (2008: 33); "crowding and need for major repairs more common for Métis living in rural areas" (2008: 34); "Métis more likely than non-Aboriginal people to move within the same census subdivision" (2008: 36); and "older Métis more likely to speak an Aboriginal language" (2008: 37).

Statisticians who attempt to produce empirically robust depictions of "the Métis nation" are thus forced to do so with data that severely limit their ability to do so. Certainly, proxy measures are possible—since the Métis people are from western Canada, for example, geographical location can be used as a proxy. Likewise, since Métis nation members likely hold longer standing affiliations to the identity, and since in many of these communities being Métis is linked to certain cultural activities, perhaps the Aboriginal Peoples Survey—which asks questions on many of these activities—can also be used as a proxy for Métis nationhood, but either of these pales in comparison to a specific question that would produce a more specific measure of Métis nationhood.

A more specific question emphasizing a commitment to Métis nationhood is easy enough to create, as a matter of logic. As I have written elsewhere, such a question would be something like, "Are you a member of the 'Métis Nation,' i.e., the Aboriginal people whose ancestors historically self-identified as Métis and who resided in the Historic Métis Nation Homeland of western Canada?" (Andersen 2008: 359). If census officials wanted to differentiate between those who self identified as Métis based on the belief that it referred to their mixed Aboriginal and non-Aboriginal ancestry and those who claimed allegiance to the Métis nation, they could fashion a question that placed this additional query below the question framed earlier in this paragraph. Otherwise, this question could replace that one. Either way, the additional question or questions would allow for a more specific demographic analysis of "the Métis nation."

The situation is probably more complicated than I have laid it out here. For example, many experts and consultants who work for Métis organizations make use of the larger numbers to make additional claims to resources. When the Métis population increased by 50 percent between 1996 and 2001, for example, the Métis National Council used that statistic as leverage to call for more funding and resources for Métis specific programs (see Andersen 2008: 364). On the other hand, government officials have not validated the doubling of the Métis population between 1996 and 2006, continuing to formulate their NARAM formulas (discussed in Chapter 1) using 1996 Métis population levels. As such, none of the increases in 2001 and 2006 are reflected in the population portion of the formula.

Ultimately, demographically speaking it does not matter how respectful Statistics Canada or other government agencies are of Métis national aspirations. As long as the census questions they ask fail to differentiate between racialized and nationalist expressions of Métis self-identification, the outcome for the Métis remains negative. Empirical depictions of nation are critically important to naturalizing various kinds of political claims. Urla (1993) demonstrates that in the Basque region of Spain, for example, Basque nationalists used census measures of Basque language decline as a means of making political claims for Basque nationhood. The point, in this context, is not their use of the census itself but, rather, that a clear question existed through which they could make such claims. Failing to make changes to the current census question for delineating the "Métis population" will seriously complicate the ability of the Métis to enumerate themselves into "empirical reality" and, therefore, to make the kinds of claims to government that only such apparently natural depictions allow.

Conclusion

This chapter has focused on the ways in which officially conceived data like that produced through the census create technically accurate but narrowly conceived statistical configurations of Aboriginal sociality in Canada that remain deeply indebted to development-based and racialized models of policy. This narrowness is somewhat mitigated by Statistics Canada's creation and use of the Aboriginal Peoples Survey, but nonetheless, the categories of "identity" to which the various indicators of socio-demographic status are cross-tabulated constrict or limit our "statistical imagination" in ways unhelpful for thinking more broadly about our sociality. Thus, in a very real way current dominant trends in Aboriginal statistics are writing out alternative (and, in many cases, more positive) stories about Aboriginality that potentially sit in stark contrast to the stories told using official data.

Bearing this in mind, in the chapter's third part we explored the complexity and distinctiveness of growing urban Aboriginal communities. We explained how, even in cases like an Aboriginal Peoples Survey containing hundreds of questions relating to various aspects of our sociality, its exploration remains limited by the policy priorities of those funding the survey (in this case, government agencies prioritizing Aboriginal issues in general, health, and employment and training). The chapter then briefly discussed the creation of Edmonton's Wicihitowin process and their inclusion of a statistical component in their "Indigenous methods." We find this to be a welcome inclusion and one that demonstrated the utility of statistical methods while still allowing for a research process endogamous to the research priorities and relations of the city of Edmonton.

Ultimately, it is unlikely that processes like Wichitowin will ever replace longer standing data sources like the census. However, the process's workbook surveys reveal a statistical configuration related to the kinds of information produced through the census yet still distinctive within the policy priorities of Edmonton's urban Aboriginal community. Generations of a failure of federal government leadership in Canada means that provinces and municipalities have stepped into the policy gap in ways that have rendered urban Aboriginal populations highly vernacular by city (see Andersen and Strachan 2012). Edmonton's Wichitowin process reflects that vernacularity, and, indeed, the policy priorities it identified and the statistical information it generated in their wake do as well. We think that statistical configurations like those generated through Wicihowin offer an important alternative to those produced through the census, ones far more attentive to the community's immediate priorities.

Finally, the chapter explored the racialization of Métis identity in the Canadian census, demonstrating how the lack of official interest in enumerating Métis, which began more than a century ago after our political demise in 1885, continues to stymie attempts to create empirical depictions of Métis nationhood. This is deeply problematic not least because, as we have pointed out throughout the book, statistics offer an elementally powerful form of legitimacy that can buttress up related political claims. Despite the fact that data are socially constructed, they often function as a "thing" that political and policy actors can hold up and say, "See? Here's what it looks like." A Métis national ontology is Indigenous no less than the ontology of any tribally specific grouping. Nonetheless, current census configurations muddy the waters and thus erase the contours of what that ontology might look like in empirical practice.

Notes

1 Since this chapter is discussing the experiences of Chris Andersen, the first person "I" is used.

2 So, for example, instead of asking what language is associated with the respondent's ethnic affiliation, the current National Household Survey asks a number of questions regarding what language, other than English or French, the respondent is competent in and what language was spoken in the home.

3 This is due to explicit Canadian policies meant to keep Aboriginal people out of (and in certain cases remove them from) urban contexts. See Peters and Andersen (in press) for a comparative discussion of Indigenous urbanization in Canada, Australia, New Zealand, and the United States.

4 Fact Sheet—Urban Aboriginal population in Canada. www.aadnc-aandc.gc.ca/eng/1100100014298/1100100014302 (accessed March 3, 2012).

5 For a broad overview of the history of Aboriginal urbanization in Canada, see Peters (2011).

6 One recent Canadian report suggests that urban Aboriginal communities remain centered around institutions wedded to development-based policies (social service delivery, and so forth). Middle-class urban Aboriginals may not recognize their urban Aboriginal "selves" in this context and, over time, may come to feel alienated from it. Intergenerationally, this impacts the contours of the urban Aboriginal community itself. From a family perspective, it might also impact the kinds of identity choices their children are likely to make in situations where, due to the impact of these feelings of alienation on their parents, they grow up in an urban community but not within an urban Aboriginal one.

7 www23.statcan.gc.ca/imdb-bmdi/instrument/3250_Q10_V1-eng.htm.

8 Aboriginal Peoples Survey: instrument design. www.statcan.gc.ca/cgi-bin/imdb/p2SV.pl?Function=getSurvey&SDDS=3250&lang=en&db=imdb&adm=8&dis=2 (accessed March 3, 2012).

9 OFI is an internal arm of the larger Aboriginal Affairs and Northern Development (AAND), which was primarily responsible for "Indian" policy in Canada. AAND was formerly known as INAC or Indian Affairs and Northern Development but underwent a recent title change to the apparently more inclusive title it sports today.

10 Edmonton is the capital of the province of Alberta, located in western Canada. With a Census Metropolitan Area (CMA) population of over a million, it has the second largest urban Aboriginal population in Canada, at more than 50,000.

11 wicihitowin.ca/history (accessed March 4, 2012).

12 wicihitowin.ca/action-circles (accessed March 4, 2012).

13 www.edmonton.ca/city_government/documents/PDF/YCYV_report.pdf (accessed March 4, 2012).

Chapter 6

Conclusion
Indigenous Peoples and Statistics

Introduction

We conclude our book with a discussion of the importance of building what we term "statistical literacy" among first world Aboriginal nations, communities, and researchers. By statistical literacy we refer, first, to understanding in terms of the categories used to collect, analyze, interpret, and use Indigenous data relating to our own peoples within our own nation-states. Second, and perhaps more urgently, we refer to the need to massively build the practice and production of statistical analysis under our own tent. We hope we have demonstrated in the previous five chapters the utility of our Indigenous quantitative methodological approach to guide Indigenous researchers towards both these ends. Certainly, statistical literacy has already begun to take hold in certain areas of the world (such as Aotearoa New Zealand) but, by and large, this remains the exception rather than the rule.

Indigenous Statistical Resistance

Quantitative research appears to have a significant image problem within Indigenous research circles. Not only are there very few Indigenous practitioners of quantitative research, but, as articulated in Chapter 3, for many researchers the concept of quantitative methodology itself is viewed as anathema to appropriate Indigenous research practice. Quantitative work is seen as both foreign and as the epitome of colonizer settler research methodology in action—a view that positions Indigenous methodologies and quantitative research as fundamentally incommensurable and, as such, to be either critiqued or avoided all-together.

Indigenous Statistics: A Quantitative Research Methodology by Maggie Walter and Chris Andersen,
130–136. © 2013 Left Coast Press, Inc. All rights reserved.

Active resistance to, or lack of interest in, quantitative research by Indigenous researchers is understandable. Indigenous peoples in first world nations are well aware that there is little to support a claim that settler scientific research paradigms—like those found in statistical research—operate in the interests of Indigenous people. Our experiences underpin the broad array of factors preventing greater engagement of Indigenous researchers with quantitative research. Perhaps the most significant of these is the historical link between quantitative research practice and science aligned research models. Such models, imbued with the positivist belief that scientific method can discover an underlying and "objective" social reality, led to the type of research that has resulted in the longstanding, widespread, and, in many cases, justifiable research suspicion among Indigenous people and communities.

We have had to, and continue to have to, endure the analysis, theorization about, and problematization of our cultures and lives by researchers working within these methodological paradigms. And while the introduction of Indigenous specific ethical rules and guidelines across our various first world nation-states has reduced some of the more flagrant abuses, the sins of the past continue to shape Indigenous attitudes toward research. Our elders still remember being measured and prodded, and their details recorded by a seeming endless stream of anthropologists (see, for example, Mallett 2002) more interested in their utility as unique specimens than as human beings, and the hurt remains (Walter 2005).

Many sins of the past also remain unremedied. Indigenous peoples from Anglo settler nation-states remain locked in the ongoing battle to return our ancestors and their funereal artifacts from overseas museums and universities home to country. Moreover, not all research wrongs remain in the past. As demonstrated in the previous two chapters, research continues to produce, from colonizer settler quantitative methodological frameworks, politically and racialized "findings" that reflect and further the interests of the settler colonizing majority. In Canada, Australia, the United States, and Aotearoa New Zealand, these analyses continue to buttress, authorize, legitimize, and institutionalize the perception of Indigenous peoples as the deficit "other" within the dominant discourse of population statistics. Research, especially that aligned with a science based empiricist model and linked to a rationalist framework, is inextricably linked to European imperialism and colonialism (Tuhiwai Smith 1999).

Methodologies, Not Methods, Injure

And so it is that statistical analysis gets positioned in tension with Indigenous knowledge. As such, attempts to craft alternatives to the dominant and/or state-sponsored study of Indigenous peoples has largely rooted itself, we would argue somewhat irrationally, in opposition to statistical analysis. Indeed, if Tuhiwai Smith (1999) is correct and "research" has become a dirty word in

Indigenous communities, much of this tends to be *statistical* research, part of a larger critique of the scientific method. As one Indigenous researcher during the early 1990s put it:

> Most statistics do not accurately represent the reality of Native communities. Although Indigenous communities have been studied, health data are collected by federal officials and with little consistence in collection methods. Cultural barriers often complicate data collection and interpretation. In addition, urban Natives are either not identified or are not part of mainstream research. (McAffee 1992, in Gilchrist 1997: 70)

A text of this length cannot do justice to a century of statistical research on Indigenous communities, and any conclusions drawn will necessarily be schematic. Nevertheless, we believe that McAffee's (1992) interpretation of dominant trends in quantitative research on Indigenous communities is largely correct and that the statement remains as true today as it did when it was made. However, though this is often positioned as a fatal flaw in the collection of statistical information *in toto*, we argue here that what is actually being described is a specific context of power within which statistics have traditionally been collected. Moreover, we argue that this is the result of a situation in which Indigenous experts and organizations have little control over the categories employed to measure narrow slices of our social complexity. The answer to our lack of control is not to remove ourselves from the methodological stage: it is, instead, to equip ourselves to retake at least some of the terrain, to turn into Indigenous space what is usually understood—by whites and Indigenous peoples alike—as white space.

The fractured relationship between first world Indigenous people and research is problematic for Indigenous peoples and researchers in ways not typically experienced by first world non-Indigenous peoples and researchers (though this observation is obviously tempered in a number of ways, including by class and heteronormativity). As Indigenous peoples, many of us have internalized our peoples' resistance and therefore are not immune from aversive responses to research practice. However, this research negativity is not indiscriminate. Rather, it seems to attach itself to quantitative research in a way not mirrored in Indigenous responses to qualitative research practice, despite the fact that both research methodologies are located in the social field of academia. As discussed in Chapter 3, this may be because qualitative research methodologies, via their non-numerical and therefore seemingly softer formats, have tended to be judged to be in some way more amenable to Indigenous research practice, despite their similar culpability in past (and present) research wrongs and simplicities (Walter 2005). Such assumptions are wrong in their less-than-critical adoption of qualitative methods, but more importantly in terms of their overcritical, and less than well-informed, dismissal of quantitative methods.

Thus, we find the juxtaposition of quantitative methods with tainted settler research paradigms fundamentally wrong-headed. Perceived ties between damaging research practices and quantitative methods are seen to align with the colonizer settler obsession of calculating and quantifying. That is, the seemingly unshakable reputation of quantitative research as embodying all that is wrong with research is largely built around a misplaced conflation of statistical techniques and processes within colonizer settler framed quantitative methodology with the method itself. Since colonization, this methodology and its purveyors have been enumerating and measuring the Indigenous peoples in support of our dispossession in our "captor nations" (Chartrand 1991). But it is the methodology, not the methods, that framed how this counting was used to first estimate the level of threat we posed to colonizing intentions, later to predict and confirm our apparent extinction, and contemporaneously to pejoratively compare us with the normalized majority.

As we have shown in this book, the strength of statistical analysis and techniques can and should be retained and positioned within an Indigenous quantitative methodology. Further, to reject quantitative work on the basis of the bad methodological company it has traditionally kept is at best pointless and at worst—and we believe there is a strong argument for worst case—harmful. The effects of the pejorative investment of our social relations in statistical form by generations of government policy makers cannot be levelled or balanced by a refusal to participate in the research arena in which these data are constructed. All such a refusal does is ensure that the guilty methodological frames and practices remain unchallenged as the "normal" quantitative methodologies.

Another factor in the mistrust of quantitative research is the fact that the field remains a largely Indigenous-free zone. As detailed in Chapter 1, although Indigenous peoples are the subject of census and administrative collections around the health, welfare, and justice systems, it is largely non-Indigenous researchers undertaking research using these data. This is not to suggest a deliberate exclusion of Indigenous people or researchers. Statistics Bureaus in both Australia and Canada have developed Indigenous community engagement strategies over the last decade or so. But the major collection agencies in neither country have actively succeeded in engaging Indigenous researchers more meaningfully in how and why Indigenous data are collected and analyzed. This lack of an established Indigenous presence, combined with the specific and technical language used and the statistical basis of quantitative analysis create an atmosphere around the practice that is alien to many Indigenous researchers.

The Power of Data

A common response to our exhortation to Indigenous researchers to become more statistically skilled is the claim that research done "our way" (that is, qualitatively) is as useful. But attempting to compete using non-quantitative techniques misses the essential point that statistical information will be collected, analyzed, and disseminated by our respective nation-states and by our respective colonizing settler researchers with or without our involvement. If Indigenous researchers do not undertake quantitative research in areas of pressing concern for Indigenous people, we can be very sure that others will. And it will be their questions that get posed, their interpretations of the analysis that influence, and their prioritizations that drive research and policy (Walter 2005).

Even more critically from a policy context, statistical results will almost always count for more than qualitatively obtained evidence. We underestimate the power of the data in our colonizing settler first world nations at our peril. From a political perspective, the results of such analyses are effective in influencing the influential. Such quantitative "proof" is fundamental to advancing a convincing case for much needed social and political change. The social and political acceptance of the validity of statistical analysis makes these techniques powerful purveyors of an Indigenous research agenda. We point to the Indigenous quantitative methodology framed research example outlined in Chapters 4 and 5 to demonstrate the acceptance of statistics as "real" evidence within our respective states. While the findings of these research projects have not always proven politically palatable to some of our critics, the essential validity of the findings has not been queried.

Our point here is not that the results were necessarily startling. Rather, that the fact that these results can be "proved" in statistical terms means that they are taken seriously in a way that qualitative findings are not. The reason for this less problematic acceptance is again the settler obsession with measuring and quantifying as a way of making social phenomena not just understandable but *real*. This belief system can be used to position the validity and consequences of our research. In turn, the quantitative mantle of legitimacy can support our drive for an Indigenous prioritized research agenda.

Our essential point is that if, as Indigenous researchers, we want our research to be effective in achieving positive change and direct benefits for our people and communities, then we need to be able to confidently use research tools and methods that are both valued and deemed valid within the political and policy spheres where such changes can be made. Hence, Indigenous communities *must* become literate in the entire statistical cycle of the construction, collection, interpretation, and dissemination of quantitative information. Increasing our statistical literacy can open the possibility of levelling the relations of power within which statistical information is accorded its legitimacy in a manner that refusal or replacement with qualitative research cannot.

Harnessing the power of the data into our research framework opens us, as Indigenous scholars, to a wider world of research possibilities as well as opening up the world of research to the wider practice to Indigenous methodologies. As Martin (2003: 1) notes, "It would be illogical to presume one research paradigm could be applicable to all research paradigms." We need to access *all* research areas to maximize our research relevancy. Quantitative techniques and statistical literacy are part of opening that door. Winch and Hayward (1999, cited in Humphrey 2001: 199) extend our understanding of accessing all areas of research to utilizing the full range of Western methods, as well as our own. Rather than reject all that is colonizer settler in origin, they argue that we can treat "Coloniser settler research traditions as a 'toolbox' from which to take methods deemed appropriate to Aboriginal knowledge production, and insisting on the development of new paradigms of research governed by 'Aboriginal Terms of Reference.'" Essentially, methods are tools to collect data, and in the social sciences, the vast majority of research methods, Western and Indigenous, are just different ways of using human communication processes to reflect, measure, or describe social processes. And as tools, they are adaptable and malleable. As such, they can almost always be utilized effectively within an Indigenous methodological framework.

Active Participants or Enclaved Specialists?

If we operate within a restricted range of research practice, we effectively become enclaved within an Indigenous-only research space: marginalized from, segregated from, and, as we believe is increasingly obvious, patronized by the broader world of scholarly and policy related research. We build the walls of our own isolation, constructing a research terrain in which we might feel comfortable and secure, but from which we are unable to challenge or even engage those outside this realm as peers. All of us who work within or with research know the dangers here. Via our comparative lack of formal research qualifications like PhDs, for many years we have been constrained to the role of "helpers" of academically qualified white colonizser settler researchers. We need to be leaders, not helpers.

This colonizer settler determination of the proper/standard Aboriginal role regarding research into our various peoples, communities, and populations has played out in academia as well as within our communities. Our presence has legitimized and authorized their research, given them entrée to our communities and families, and built and funded their academic careers. And all for the price of casual employment (at best, many times such services were/are expected to be provided *gratis*; they are, after all, helping us), or if we were lucky, the inclusion of our name at the end of a list of authors of reports or papers over which we had no control, and which made little substantive contribution to, and even less benefit for, ourselves or our communities. Now that our various peoples are increasingly gaining the academic skills and qualifications to initiate and conduct research in our own right, we should not squander our new powers by re-restricting ourselves to just a small portion of the research stage: doing so handicaps ourselves and our peoples.

Such restrictive research practices also play to the interests of that group of colonizer settler researchers who, having built a career studying and researching Indigenous peoples with impunity, now perceive our newly found capacities as researchers threatening and ontologically disturbing. This critique does not, of course, encompass all non-Indigenous researchers in the field. Many have played a critical role in assisting our research capacity building and support Indigenous research agendas. For that we thank them and want to continue to work in partnership. But all of us working in Indigenous research know of many who do not support our agendas. Occupying the field, if not also the tiny spaces we have been granted within universities and the higher education sector, they are reluctant to give way, or even create room, for Indigenous researchers and Indigenous methodologies. Their presence retards, rather than assists, our efforts to build Indigenous capacity, scholarship, and endeavors to engage our communities as partners and colleagues, not subjects.

In effect, the Indigenous research terrain has been colonized, and the occupiers are not to be dislodged easily. But these are not simply settlers, they are squatters. And as Indigenous peoples, communities, and researchers we do not need to seek new research territories but to demand the equivalent of research land rights to the research country of which *we* are the traditional and the modern owners. The legitimacy of our claims to such research country relies on our capacity to demonstrate that we can, and do, use the terrain wisely and well. Quantitative research methodologies, the research practices they engender, and the skills base to interpret and use them are central to validating our declarations of research self-determination.

References

ABS. 2007. *Directions in Australia's Aboriginal and Torres Strait Islander Statistics.* Canberra: Australian Bureau of Statistics.

———. 2010. Population Characteristics of Aboriginal and Torres Strait Islander Australians. 2006. Cat. No. 4713.0. Australian Bureau of Statistics: Canberra.

Aboriginal Affairs and Northern Development. Fact Sheet: Urban Aboriginal population in Canada. www.aadnc-aandc.gc.ca/eng/1100100014298/1100100014302 (accessed March 3, 2012).

Acker, S. 2000. In/out/side: Positioning the researcher in feminist qualitative research. *Resources for Feminist Research* 28(1/2): 189–210.

Adler, P., and P. Adler. 1987. *Membership roles in field research.* Newbury Park, CA: Sage.

AIHW. 2008. *The Health and Welfare of Australia's Aboriginal and Torres Strait Islander Peoples,* Cat. No. 4704.0. Canberra: Australian Bureau of Statistics.

———. 2011a. *The Health and Welfare of Australia's Aboriginal and Torres Strait Islander Peoples,* Cat. No. 4704.0. Canberra: Australian Bureau of Statistics.

———. 2011b. Comparing life expectancy of indigenous people in Australia, New Zealand, Canada and the United States: Conceptual, methodological and data issues. www.aihw. gov.au/indigenous-observatory-international-comparisons/ (accessed March 3, 2013).

Altman, J., N. Biddle, and B. Hunter. 2008, *How realistic are the prospects for closing the gaps in socioeconomic outcomes for Indigenous Australians?* Canberra: Centre for Aboriginal Economic Policy Research, Australian National University.

Altman, J. C., and J. Taylor. 1996. Statistical needs in Indigenous affairs: Future options and implications. In J. C. Altman and J. Taylor (eds.), *The 1994 National Aboriginal and Torres Strait islander survey: Findings and future prospects* (pp. 193–202). Canberra: Centre for Aboriginal Economic Policy Research, Australian National University.

Andersen, C. 2008. From nation to population: The racialization of 'Métis' in the Canadian census. *Nations and Nationalism* 14(2):347–368.

———. 2009. Critical Indigenous studies: From difference to density. *Cultural Studies Review* 15(2):97–115.

———. 2011. *moya 'tipimsook* ('the people who aren't their own bosses'): Racialization and the misrecognition of Métis in upper Great Lakes ethnohistory. *Ethnohistory* 58(1):37–63.

———. 2013a. Urban Aboriginality as distinctive, in twelve parts. In E. Peters and C. Andersen (eds.), *Indigenous identities and urbanization in international perspective: Cultural resilience and innovation in four settler nations* (pp. 46–68). Vancouver, BC: UBC Press.

———. 2013b. From ethnic to categorical mobility: Challenging conventional demographic explanations of Métis population growth. In F. Trovato and A. Romaniuc (eds.), *Aboriginal demography in transition* (pp. 276–298). Edmonton: University of Alberta Press.

———. In press. Underdeveloped identities: The misrecognition of Aboriginality in the Canadian census. *Economy & Society.*

———, and J. Strachan. 2012. Urban Aboriginal policy in a coordination vacuum: The Alberta (dis)advantage. In E. Peters (ed.), *Fields of governance 2: Making urban Aboriginal policy in Canadian municipalities* (pp. 127–159). Montreal: McGill-Queen's University Press.

Anderson, B. 1991. *Imagined communities: Reflections on the origin and spread of nationalism* (revised and enlarged edition). London: Verso.

Anzaldua, G. 1987. *Borderlands / la frontera: The new mestiza.* San Francisco: Spinsters/Aunt Lute.

APS (Aboriginal Peoples Survey). 2012. Aboriginal Peoples Survey. Ottawa: Statistics Canada (in text as APS 2012). www.statcan.gc.ca/cgi-bin/imdb/p2SV.pl?Function=getSurvey&SDDS=3250&lang=en&db=imdb&adm=8&dis=2 (accessed March 3, 2012).

ASSDA. n.d. *Section 1 introduction: Census.* assda.anu.edu.au/census/c86/hatac86/section 1.html (accessed March 19, 2013).

Atkinson, R., E. Taylor, and M. Walter. 2010. Burying Indigeneity: The spatial construction of reality and Aboriginal Australia. *Social and Legal Studies* 19(2):313–330.

Attwood, B. 1992. Introduction. In B. Attwood and J. Arnold (eds.), *Power, knowledge and Aborigines* (pp. i–xvi). Melbourne: La Trobe University Press in association with the National Centre for Australian Studies.

———, and A. Markus. 1999. *The struggle for Aboriginal rights: A documentary history.* Crows Nest, Australia: Allen and Unwin.

AuSSA. 2007. *The Australian Survey of Social Attitudes, AuSSA Data.* The Australian Demographic & Social Research Institute (ADSRI), Australian National University, College of Arts & Social Sciences. aussa.anu.edu.au/data.php (accessed November 11, 2008).

Axelsson, R., and P. Skold. eds. 2011. *Indigenous peoples and demography: The complex relation between identity and statistics.* New York: Beghahn Books.

Babbie, E. 2007. *The basics of social research*, 2nd Edition. Southbank, Australia: Thomson, Wadsworth.

Barry, A., T. Osborne, and N. Rose. 1996. *Foucault and political reason: Liberalism, neo-liberalism and rationalities of government.* London: UCL Press.

Battiste, M. 2008. Research ethics for protecting Indigenous knowledge and heritage: Institutional and researcher responsibilities. In N. K. Denzin., Y. S. Lincoln, and L. Tuhiwai Smith (eds.), *Handbook of critical and Indigenous methodologies* (pp. 497–510). Thousand Oaks, CA: Sage.

———, and J. Henderson. 2000. *Protecting Indigenous knowledge and heritage.* Saskatoon, SK: Purich.

Bessarab, D., and B. Ng'andu. 2010. Yarning about yarning as a legitimate method in Indigenous research. *International Journal of Critical Indigenous Studies* 3(1):37–50.

Bishop, R. 2008. Te Kotahitanga: Kaupapa Maori in mainstream classrooms. In N. K. Denzin., Y. S. Lincoln, and L. Tuhiwai Smith (eds.), *Handbook of critical and Indigenous methodologies* (pp. 439–458). Thousand Oaks, CA: Sage.

Blazer, M., H. A. Feit, and G. McRae. 2004. *In the way of development: Indigenous peoples, life projects and globalization.* London and New York: Zed Books.

Bonwick, J. 1969. *The last of the Tasmanians, or, The black war of Van Diemen's Land.* London: S. Low, Son & Marston, 1870. Adelaide: Libraries Board of South Australia.

Bonilla-Silva, E. 2010. *Racism without racists: Colour-blind racism and the persistence of racial inequality in America.* Lanham, MD: Rowman & Littlefield.

Bourdieu, P. 1984. *Distinction: A social critique of the judgment of taste.* London: Routledge.

———. 1991. *Language and symbolic power.* Cambridge, UK: Polity Press.

Boyd, M., G. Goldman, and P. White. 2000. Race in the Canadian census. In L. Driedger and S. Halli (eds.), *In race and racism: Canada's challenge* (pp. 33–34). Montreal and Kingston: McGill-Queen's University Press.

Brubaker, R. 2004. *Ethnicity without groups.* Cambridge, MA: Harvard University Press.

Bryman, A. 2004. *Social research methods,* 2nd Edition. Oxford: Oxford University Press.

Burnham, P., K. Gilland, W. Grant., and Z. Layton-Henry. 2004. *Research methods in politics.* Basingstoke, UK: Palgrave Macmillan.

Burshell, G. 1991. "Peculiar interests": governing the system of natural liberty. In G. Burshell, C. Gordon, and P. Miller (eds.), *The Foucault Effect: Studies in governmentality* (pp. 119–150). London: Harvester Wheatsheaf.

———, C. Gordon, and P. Miller (eds.). 1991. *The Foucault Effect: Studies in governmentality.* London: Harvester Wheatsheaf.

Cannella, G. S., and K. D. Manuelito. 2008. Feminisms from unthought locations: Indigenous worldviews, marginalised feminisms and revisioning an anticolonial social science. In N. K. Denzin., Y. S. Lincoln, and L. Tuhiwai Smith (eds.), *Handbook of critical and Indigenous methodologies* (pp. 45–60). Thousand Oaks, CA: Sage.

Casey, M. 2008. Managing resistance: Whiteness and the storytellers of Indigenous protest in Australia. In A. Moreton-Robinson, M. Casey, and F. Nicoll (eds.), *Transnational whiteness matters: Mythunderstanding* (pp. 19–38). Plymouth, UK: Lexington Books.

Cassidy, J. 2006. The stolen generations—Canada and Australia: The legacy of assimilation. *Deakin Law Review* 11(1):132–177.

Census Bureau. 2012. *American Indian and Alaska Native*. Department of Commerce. www.census.gov/aian/ (accessed March 19, 2013).

Chartrand, P. 1991. 'Terms of division': Problems of 'outside-naming' for Aboriginal people in Canada. *Journal of Indigenous Studies* 2(2):1–22.

Chatterjee, P. 1993. *A nation and its fragments: Colonial and postcolonial histories*. Princeton, NJ: Princeton University Press.

Chesterman, J., and B. Galligan. 1997. *Citizens without rights*. Cambridge, UK: Cambridge University Press.

Chilisa, B. 2012. *Indigenous research methodologies*. Los Angeles: Sage.

Chretien, J. 2011 [1969]. *Statement of the Government of Canada on Indian Policy, 1969 (The White Paper, 1969)*. Ottawa: Government of Canada.

Closing the Gap: Prime Ministers's Report 2013. Canberra: Australian Government.

Collier, T. O., Jr. 1998. *Supervisors guide to labor relations*. Alexandria, VA: Society for Human Resource Management.

Connell, R. 2007. *Southern theory: The global dynamics of knowledge in social science*. Sydney: Allen and Unwin.

Cooke, M., F. Mitrou, D. Lawrence, E. Guimond, and D. Beavon. 2007. Indigenous well-being in four countries: An application of the UNDP'S Human Development Index to Indigenous peoples in Australia, Canada, New Zealand, and the United States. *BMC International Health and Human Rights* 7(9):1–11.

Cook-Lynn E. 1998. American Indian studies: An overview. Keynote Address at the Native Studies Conferences, Yale University, February 5, 1998. *Wicazo Sa Review* 14(2):14–24.

———. 2008. History, myth and identity in the new Indian story. In N. K. Denzin., Y. S. Lincoln, and L. Tuhiwai Smith (eds.), *Handbook of critical and Indigenous methodologies* (pp. 329–346). Thousand Oaks, CA: Sage.

Cottrell, M. 2010. Indigenous education in comparative perspective: Global opportunities for reimagining schools. *International Journal for Cross-Disciplinary Subjects in Education* 1(4):223–227.

Curtis, B. 2001. *The politics of population: State formation, statistics and the census of Canada*. Toronto: University of Toronto Press.

Day, R. 2000. *Multiculturalism and the history of Canadian diversity*. Toronto: University of Toronto Press.

Dean, M. 2010. *Governmentality: Power and rule in modern society*. London: Sage.

DEEWR. 2008. *National Report to Parliament on Indigenous Education and Training, 2006*. Department of Education, Employment and Workplace Relations: Canberra, Australia.

Deloria, V., Jr. 1997. *Indians and anthropologists: Vine Deloria, Jr., and the critique of anthropology*. T. Biolsi and L. J. Zimmerman (eds.). Tuscon: University of Arizona Press.

———, and D. Wildcat. 2001. *Power and place*. Golden, CO: Fulcrum.

Denis, C. 1997. *We are not you: First Nations and Canadian modernity*. Peterborough, ON: Broadview Press.

Denzin, N. K., and Y. S. Lincoln. 2008. Introduction. In N. K. Denzin., Y. S. Lincoln, and L. Tuhiwai Smith (eds.), *Handbook of critical and Indigenous methodologies* (pp. 1–20). Thousand Oaks, CA: Sage.

Desai, V., and R. Potter. 2002. *The companion to development studies.* Oxford: Oxford University Press.

Dickason, O. 1992. *Canada's First Nations: A history of founding peoples from earliest times.* Toronto: McClelland and Stewart.

Dudgeon, P., K. Cox, D. D'Anna, C. Dunkely, K. Hams, K. Kelly, C. Scrine, and R. Walker. 2012. *Hear our voices: Community consultations for the development of an empowerment, healing and leadership program for Aboriginal people living in the Kimberley, Western Australia.* Canberra: Commonwealth of Australia.

Dunn, K., F. Forrest, I. Burnley, and A. McDonald. 2004. Constructing racism in Australia. *Australian Journal of Social Issues* 394:409–430.

Dyck, N. 1985. *Indigenous peoples and the nation-state: 'Fourth world' politics in Canada, Australia, and Norway.* St. Johns, NL: Institute of Social and Economic Research.

Eberts, M. 2010. McIvor: Justice delayed—again. *Indigenous Law Journal* 9:15–46.

Ens, G. 1996. *Homeland to hinterland: The changing worlds of the Red River Metis in the nineteenth century.* Toronto: University of Toronto Press.

Evans, M., A. Miller, P. Hutchinson, and C. Dingwall. Forthcoming. De-colonizing research practice: Indigenous methodologies, Aboriginal methods, and knowledge/knowing. In P. Leavy (ed.), *Oxford handbook of qualitative research.* New York: Oxford University Press.

Ezzy, D. 2002. *Qualitative analysis.* Sydney: Allen and Unwin.

Fact Sheet. 2010. Urban Aboriginal population in Canada. www.aadnc-aandc.gc.ca/eng/1100100014298/1100100014302 (accessed March 3, 2012).

FAHCSIA. 2012. *Stronger futures in the Northern Territory.* Federal Department of Families, Housing Community Services and Indigenous Affairs. www.fahcsia.gov.au/our-responsibilities/indigenous-australians/programs-services/stronger-futures-in-the-northern-territory-0 (accessed March 19, 2013).

Firestone, S. 1972. *The dialectic of sex.* London: Paladin.

Fonseca, F. 2012. *Census releases data on American Indian population.* YAHOO! NEWS January 26. news.yahoo.com/census-releases-data-american-indian-population-205256402.html (accessed March 19, 2013).

Foucault, M. 1972. *The archaeology of knowledge and the discourse on language.* London: Routledge.

———. 1991. On governmentality. In G. Burshell, C. Gordon, and P. Miller (eds.), *The Foucault Effect: Studies in governmentality* (pp. 87–104). London: Harvester Wheatsheaf.

Frankenberg, R. 1993. *The social construction of whiteness: White women, race matters.* London: Routledge.

Gilchrist, L. 1997. Aboriginal communities and social science research: Voyeurism in translation. *Native Social Work Journal* 1(1):69–85.

Goot, M., and I. Watson. 2001. One nation's electoral support: Where does it come from, what makes it different and how does it fit? *Australian Journal of Politics and History* 47(2):159–191.

Goot, M., and T. Rowse. 2007. *Divided nation: Indigenous affairs and the imagined public.* Melbourne: Melbourne University Press.

Gordon, M. 2011. NT welfare to be tied to school attendance. *The Age* (October 18). www. theage.com.au/national/nt-welfare-to-be-tied-to-school-attendance-20111017-1ltcc. html (accessed March 19, 2013).

Graham K., and E. Peters. 2002. *Aboriginal communities and urban sustainability.* Ottawa: Canadian Policy Research Network.

Grande, S. 2008. Red pedagogy: The un-methodology. In N. K. Denzin., Y. S. Lincoln, and L. Tuhiwai Smith (eds.), *Handbook of critical and Indigenous methodologies* (pp. 217–232). Thousand Oaks, CA: Sage.

Hall, S. 1995. Introduction. In S. Hall, D. Held, D. Hubert, and K. Thompson (eds.), *Modernity: An introduction to modern societies* (pp. 3–18). Cambridge, UK: Polity Press.

Hamilton, M. 2007. 'Anyone not on the list might as well be dead': Aboriginal peoples and the censuses of Canada, 1851–1916. *Journal of the Canadian Historical Association* 18:57–79.

Hart, M. 2010. Indigenous worldviews, knowledge, and research: The development of an Indigenous research paradigm. *Journal of Indigenous Voices in Social Work* 1(1):1–16.

Havemann, P. 1999. *Indigenous peoples' rights in Australia, Canada and New Zealand.* Melbourne: Oxford University Press.

Hawthorn, H. B., ed. 1966. *A survey of the contemporary Indians of Canada: Economic, political, educational needs and policies.* Ottawa: Indian Affairs Branch.

Hayward, J. 2010. Indigenous political representation and comparative research. In B. Hokuwhitu, N. Kermoal, C. Andersen, A. Petersen, M. Reiglly, I. Altamirano-Jimenez, and P. Rewi (eds.), *Indigenous identity and resistance: Researching the diversity of knowledge* (pp. 139–150). Dunedin, New Zealand: Otago University Press.

Hindess, B. 2001. The liberal government of unfreedom. *Alternatives* 26:93–111.

———. 2004. Liberalism—what's in a name? In W. Larner and W. Walters (eds.), *Global governmentality: Governing international spaces* (pp. 23–38). London and New York: Routledge.

———. 2008. Been there, done that. *Postcolonial Studies* 11:201–213.

Hogeveen, B. R. 1999. An intrusive and corrective government: Political rationalities and the governance of plains Aboriginals 1870–1890. In R. Smandych (ed.), *Governable places: Readings on governmentality and crime control* (pp. 287–312). Aldershot, UK: Dartmouth.

Hokowhitu, B. 2009. Indigenous existentialism and the body. *Cultural Studies Review* 15(2):101–118.

Howard, S., L. Newman, V. Harris, and J. Harcourt. 2002. Talking about youth participation—where, when and why? Paper presented at *Australian Association of Research in Education Conference*, December 2–5, University of Queensland, Brisbane, Australia.

HRSDC (Human Resources and Skills Development Canada). 2004. *National Aboriginal Resource Allocation Model (NARAM) Workshop*. July 28–20. Ottawa, Ontario.

Humphery, K. 2001. Dirty questions: Indigenous health and "Western research." *Australian and New Zealand Journal of Public Health* 25(3):197–202.

Inwood, K., and M. Hamilton. 2011. The Aboriginal population and the 1891 Census of Canada. In P. Axelsson and P. Sköld (eds.), *Indigenous peoples and demography: The complex relation between identity and statistics* (pp. 95–116). Oxford and New York: Berghahn Books.

ISSR. 2012. *Responding to Indigenous homelessness*. Institute of Social Science Research, St Lucia: The University of Queensland. www.issr.uq.edu.au/news/responding-indigenous-homelessness (accessed March 29, 2013).

Ivison, D., P. Patton, and W. Sanders, eds. 2000. *Political theory and the rights of Indigenous peoples*. Cambridge, UK: Cambridge University Press.

Jackson, N. O. 2008. Educational attainment and the (growing) importance of age structure: Indigenous and non-Indigenous Australians. *Journal of Population Research* 25(2):223–244.

Jacobs. K. 2010. Discourse analysis. In M. Walter (ed.), *Social research methods* (pp. 351–376). Melbourne: Oxford University Press.

Jones, G. 2004. The demography of disadvantage. *Journal of Population Research* 21:107–126.

Kahakalau, K. 2004. Indigenous heuristic action research: Bridging Western and Indigenous research methodologies. *Hulili: Multidisciplinary Research on Hawaiian Well-Being* 1(1):19–33.

Keen, I. 1999. Land, Rights, Laws: Issues of Native Title. *Issues paper no. 28. Native title Research Unit*, Canberra: Australian Institute of Aboriginal and Torres Strait Islander Studies.

Kelley, R. 1997. *Yo' mama's disfunktional!: Fighting the culture wars in urban America*. Boston: Beacon Press Books.

Kerbo, H. R. 1981. Characteristics of the poor: A continuing focus of social research. *Sociology and Social Research* 65:323–331.

Kerr, D., E. Guimond, and M. J. Norris. 2003. Perils and pitfalls of Aboriginal demography: Lessons learned from the Royal Commission on Aboriginal Peoples projections. In J. White, P. Masim, and D. Beavon (eds.), *Aboriginal conditions: The research foundations for public policy* (pp. 39–62). Vancouver, BC: UBC Press.

Kidwell, C. S. 2009. American Indian studies: Intellectual navel-gazing or academic discipline? *American Indian Quarterly* 33(1):1–18.

Kothari, U. 2005. *A radical history of development studies: Individuals, institutions and ideologies.* London: Zed Books.

Kovach, M. 2009. *Indigenous methodologies: Characteristics, conversations and contexts.* Toronto: University of Toronto Press.

Kukutai. T. 2011. Building ethnic boundaries in New Zealand: Representations of Maori identity in the census. In R. Axelsson and P. Skold (eds.), *Indigenous peoples and demography: The complex relation between identity and statistics* (pp. 33–54). New York: Beghahn Books.

———. 2012. Quantum Māori, Māori quantum: State constructions of Māori identities in the census, 1857/8—2006. In R. McClean, B. Patterson, and D. Swain (eds.), *Counting stories, moving ethnicities: Studies from Aotearoa New Zealand* (pp. 27–51). Hamilton, New Zealand: University of Waikato.

Langton, M. 1981. Urbanising Aborigines; the social scientists great deception. *Social Alternatives* 2(2):16–22.

Lawrence, B. 2004. *'Real' Indians and others: Mixed-blood urban native peoples and Indigenous nationhood.* Vancouver, BC: UBC Press.

Lewis, O. 1966. The culture of poverty. *Scientific American* 215:19–25.

Li, T. 2007. *The will to improve: Governmentality, development, and the practice of politics.* Durham, NC: Duke University Press.

Lipsitz, G. 2006. *The possessive investment in whiteness: How white people profit from identity politics.* Philadelphia: Temple University Press.

LSIC. 2005, Footprints in time: The longitudinal study of Indigenous children (LSIC). www.facs.gov.au/internet/facsinternet.nsf/ research/ldi-lsic_nav.htm (accessed August 1, 2005).

Macklem, P. 2001. *Indigenous difference and the Canadian Constitution.* Toronto: University of Toronto Press.

Mallett, M. 2002. *My past, their future: Stories from Cape Barren Island.* Sandy Bay, Australia: Blubber Head Press.

Martin, K. 2003. Ways of knowing, ways of being and ways of doing: A theoretical framework and methods for Indigenous re-search and Indigenist research. *Journal of Australian Studies* 76:203–214.

———. 2008. *Please knock before you enter: Aboriginal regulation of outsiders and the implications for researchers.* Teneriffe, Australia: Post Press.

Martin, D., F. Morphy, W. Sanders, and J. Taylor. 2002. *Making sense of the census: Observations of the 2001 enumeration in remote Aboriginal Australia.* Canberra, Australia: ANU E Press.

Martinez Cobo, J. R. 1987. *Study of the problem of discrimination against indigenous populations, vol. 5: Conclusions, proposals and recommendations.* New York: United Nations.

Matthews, B., and L. Ross. 2010. *Research methods: A practical guide for the social sciences.* Essex, UK: Pearson Education.

Maxim, P. S. 1999. *Quantitative research methods in social sciences*. Oxford. Oxford University Press.

McClintock, A. 1995. 'No longer in a future heaven': Gender, race, and nationalism. In A. McClintock, A. Mufti, and E. Shohat (eds.), *Dangerous liaisons: Gender, nation, and post-colonial perspectives* (pp. 89–112). Minneapolis: University of Minnesota Press.

Meyer, M. A. 2008. Indigenous and authentic: Hawaiian epistemology and the triangulation of meaning. In N. K. Denzin., Y. S. Lincoln, and L. Tuhiwai Smith (eds.), *Handbook of critical and indigenous methodologies* (pp. 89–112). Thousand Oaks, CA: Sage.

Miller, J. 1989. *Skyscrapers hide the heavens: A history of Indian-white relations in Canada*. Toronto: University of Toronto Press.

Miller, R. J., J. Ruru, L. Behrendt, and T. Lindberg. 2010. *Discovering Indigenous lands: The doctrine of discovery in the English colonies*. Oxford: Oxford University Press.

Milloy, J. 2008. *Indian Act colonialism: A century of dishonour, 1869–1969*. Research paper for the National Centre for First Nations Governance.

Mills, C. W. 1997. *The racial contract*. Ithaca, NY: Cornell University Press.

Minichiello, V., R. Aroni, E. Timewell, and L. Alexander. 1990. *In-depth interviewing: Researching people*. Melbourne: Longman Cheshire.

Moreton-Robinson, A. 2000. *Talkin up to the white woman*. Brisbane, Australia: University of Queensland Press.

———. 2004. Whiteness, epistemology and Indigenous representation. In A. Moreton-Robinson (ed.), *Whitening race* (pp. 75–88). Canberra, Australia: Aboriginal Studies Press.

———. 2006. Towards a new research agenda. *Journal of Sociology* 42(4):383–395.

———. 2008. Whiteness, epistemology and Indigenous representation. In A. Moreton-Robinson (ed.), *Whitening race* (pp. 75–88). Canberra, Australia: Aboriginal Studies Press.

———. 2006. Whiteness matters: Implications of talking up to the white woman. *Australian Feminist Studies* 21(50):245–256.

———. 2009. Imagining the good Indigenous citizen: Race war and the pathology of patriarchal white sovereignty. *Cultural Studies Review* 15(2):61–79.

———, and M. Walter. 2010. Indigenous research methodologies. In M. Walter (ed.), *Social research methods: An Australian perspective, 2nd edition*. Melbourne: Oxford. www.oup.com.au/__data/assets/pdf_file/0005/198284/Chapter_22.pdf.

———, M. Walter, D. Singh, and M. Kimber. 2011. *On Stony Ground: Governance and Aboriginal and Torres Strait Islander Participation in Australian Universities. Report to the Review of Higher Education Access and Outcomes for Aboriginal and Torres Strait Islander People*. Department of Education, Employment and Workplace Relations, Canberra, Australia.

Morphy, F., ed. 2007. *Agency, contingency and census process: Observations of the 2006 Indigenous Enumeration Strategy in remote Aboriginal Australia*. Canberra, Australia: ANU E Press.

Nakata, M. 1998. Anthropological texts and Indigenous standpoints. *Australian Aboriginal Studies Journal* 2:3–12.

NATSIS. n.d. www.abs.gov.au/ausstats/abs@.nsf/DOSSbyTopic/9AD558B6D0AED752CA 256C7600018788?OpenDocument (accessed August 24, 2012).

Neuman, W. L. 2004. *Basics of social research: Qualitative and quantitative approaches.* Boston: Pearson Education.

Nicoll, F. 2004. Reconciliation in and out of perspective: White knowing, seeing, curating and being at home in and against Indigenous sovereignty. In A. Moreton-Robinson (ed.), *Whitening race: Essays in social and cultural criticism* (pp. 17–31). Canberra, Australia: Aboriginal Studies Press.

NTEU. 2012. *Indigenous clauses: Round 5 Indigenous clauses—All agreements.* National Indigenous Unit, Melbourne, National Tertiary Education Union.

O'Sullivan, E. 2011. *The Community Well-Being Index (CWB): Measuring well-being in First Nations and non-Aboriginal communities, 1981–2006.* Unpublished report submitted to Aboriginal Affairs and Northern Development Canada.

Oakley, A. 1974. *The sociology of housework.* Oxford, UK: Blackwell.

Office of the Arts. n.d. *National indigenous languages policy.* arts.gov.au/indigenous/languages (accessed March 19, 2013).

Ortner, S. B. 1974. Is female to male as nature is to culture? In M. Z. Rosaldo and L. Pamphere (eds.), *Woman, culture and society* (pp. 67–87). Stanford, CA: Stanford University Press.

Palmater, P. 2011. *Beyond blood: Rethinking Indigenous identity.* Saskatoon, SK: Purich Press.

Pateman, C. 1991. *The sexual contract.* Cambridge, UK: Polity Press.

Peet, R., and E. Hartwick. 2009. *Theories of development, second edition: Contentions, arguments, alternatives.* New York: Guilford Press.

Peters, E. 2011. Emerging themes in academic research in urban Aboriginal identities in Canada, 1996–2010. *aboriginal policy studies* 1(1):78–105.

———, and C. Andersen, eds. 2013. *Indigenous in the city: Contemporary identities and cultural innovation.* Vancouver, BC: UBC Press.

Peterson, J. 2013. Red River redux: Métis ethnogenesis and the Great Lakes region. In N. St-Onge, C. Podruchny, and B. Macdougall (eds.), *Contours of a people: Métis family, mobility, and history* (pp. 22–58). Norman: Oklahoma University Press.

Peterson, N., and W. Sanders, eds. 1998. *Citizenship and Indigenous Australians: Changing conceptions and possibilities.* Cambridge, UK: Cambridge University Press.

Porsanger, J. 2004. *Essay about Indigenous methodology.* www.ub.uit.no/munin/ handle/10037/906 (accessed November 13, 2010).

Ray, A. 2008. *I have lived here since the world began: An illustrated history of Canada's native peoples.* Vancouver, BC: Key Porter Books.

RCAP. 1996. *Report of the Royal Commission on Aboriginal Peoples.* Five volumes. Ottawa: Minister of Supply and Services.

RCIADIC. 1991. *Royal Commission into Aboriginal Deaths in Custody.* Commonwealth of Australia, Canberra.

Reynolds, H. 1995. *Fate of a free people.* Sydney: Penguin Books.

Riggs, D. 2004. We don't talk about race anymore: Power, privilege and critical whiteness studies. *Borderlands e-journal* 3(2). www.borderlands.net.au/vol3no2_2004/riggs_intro.htm.

Rigney, L. I. 1997. Internationalisation of an Indigenous anti-colonial cultural critique of research methodologies: A guide to Indigenist research methodology and its principles, *Journal for Native American Studies* 14(12):109–121.

———. 2001. A first perspective of Indigenous Australian participation in science: Framing Indigenous research towards Indigenous Australian intellectual sovereignty. *Kaurna Higher Education Journal* 7(August):1–11.

Rose, N. 1999. *Powers of freedom: Reframing political thought.* Cambridge, UK: Cambridge University Press.

Royal Commission on Aboriginal Peoples. 1996. *Vol. 4: Perspectives and Realities.* Ottawa, ON: Minister of Supply and Services.

Ruppert, E. 2009. Becoming peoples: Counting heads in northern wilds. *Journal of Cultural Economy* 2:11–31.

Ryan, L. 1995. *The Aboriginal Tasmanians.* St Lucia, Australia: University of Queensland Press.

Saavedra, C.M., and E. D. Nymark. 2008. Borderland-*Mestizaje* feminism: The new tribalism. In N. K. Denzin., Y. S. Lincoln, and L. Tuhiwai Smith (eds.), *Handbook of critical and Indigenous methodologies* (pp. 255–276). Thousand Oaks, CA: Sage.

Sahlins, M. 1999. What is anthropological enlightenment? Some lessons of the twentieth century. *Annual Review of Anthropology* 23:i–xxii.

Said, E. 1978. *Orientalism.* New York: Knopf.

———. 1993. *Culture and imperialism.* New York: Random House.

Salée, D. 2006. Quality of life of Aboriginal people in Canada: An analysis of current research. *IIRP Choices* 12:4–36.

Scott, D. (1995). Colonial governmentality. *Social Text* 43:191–220.

Sheehan, N. 2007. Personal Communication. September 4.

Shewell, H. 2008.'Enough to keep them alive': Indian welfare in Canada, 1873–1965. Vancouver, BC: UBC Press.

Silko, L. M. 1981. Language and literature from a Pueblo Indian perspective. In L. A. Fiedler and H. A. Baker, Jr. (eds.), *English literature: Opening up the canon* (pp. 54–72). Baltimore: John Hopkins University Press.

Simmonds, S., B. Robson, F. Cram, and G. Purdie. 2008. Kaupapa Maori epidemiology. *Australasian Epidemiologist* 15(1):2–6

Simpson, A. 2008. From white into red: Captivity narratives as alchemies of race and citizenship. *American Quarterly* 60:251–257.

Stanley, G. 1992 [1960]. *The birth of Western Canada: A history of the Riel Rebellions*. Toronto: University of Toronto Press.

St-Onge, N. 2009. Plains Métis: Contours of an identity. *Australasian Canadian Studies* 27(1–2):95–115.

———, C. Podruchny, and B. Macdougall, eds. 2012. *Contours of a people: Métis family, mobility, and history*. Norman: Oklahoma University Press.

Statistics Canada. 1981. *Census Questionnaire*. Ottawa: Statistics Canada.

———. 2008. *Aboriginal Peoples in Canada in 2006: Inuit, Métis and First Nations, 2006 Census*. Ottawa: Statistics Canada.

———. 2010. *Aboriginal Peoples Technical Report, 2006 Census*. Ottawa: Statistics Canada.

Sutton, P. 2009. *The politics of suffering: Indigenous Australia and the end of the liberal consensus*. Melbourne: Melbourne University Press.

Swartz. D. 1997. *Culture and power: The sociology of Pierre Bourdieu*. Chicago: University of Chicago Press.

Taylor, J. 2004. Social indicators for Aboriginal governance insights from the Thamarrurr Region, Northern Territory. *CAEPR Monograph No. 24*, Centre for Aboriginal Economic Policy Research, The Australian National University: Canberra.

———. 2011. Beyond the pale: Measures of mobility in postcolonial Australia. *Law, Text, Culture* 15:72–99.

Tobias, J. 1991. Protection, civilization, assimilation: An outline history of Canada's Indian policy. In J. Miller (ed.), *Sweet promises: A reader on Indian-white relations in Canada* (pp. 127–144). Toronto: University of Toronto Press.

Tough, F. 1992. Aboriginal rights versus the deed of surrender: The legal rights of native peoples and Canada's acquisition of the Hudson's Bay Company territory. *Prairie Forum* 17(2):225–250.

Tuhiwai Smith, L. I. 1999. *Decolonizing methodologies, research and Indigenous peoples*. London and New York: Zed Books.

United Nations Permanent Forum on Indigenous Peoples, Indigenous People, Indigenous Voices. n.d. Who are Indigenous people? Fact Sheet. www.un.org/esa/socdev/ unpfii/ documents/5session_factsheet1.pdf (accessed November 20, 2011).

Urla, J. 1993. Cultural politics in an age of statistics: Numbers, nations, and the making of Basque identity. *American Ethnologist* 20(4):818–843.

van Krieken, R., P. Smith, D. Habibis, K. McDonald, M. Haralambos, and M. Holborn. 2000. *Sociology themes and perspectives*. Sydney: Pearson Education Australian Pty.

Wacquant, L. 1997. Three pernicious premises in the study of the American ghetto. *International Journal of Urban and Regional Research* 20(June):341–353.

Wade, L. 2012. *From appearance to identity: How the census data collection changed race in America.* thesocietypages.org/socimages/2012/12/29/from-appearance-to-identity-how-census-data-collection-changed-race-in-america/ (accessed February 2, 2013).

Walker, J. 1997. *'Race,' Rights and the Law in the Supreme Court of Canada: Historical Case Studies.* Osgoode Society for Canadian Legal History / Wilfrid Laurier Press.

Walker, R. 2008. Improving the interface between urban municipalities and Aboriginal communities. *Canadian Journal of Urban Research* 17(1):20–36.

Walter, M. 2005. Using the power of the data within Indigenous research practice. *Australian Aboriginal Studies* 2:27–34.

———. 2006. The nature of social science research. In M. Walter (ed.), *Social research methods: An Australian perspective* (pp. 1–28). Melbourne: Oxford University Press.

———. 2007. Aboriginality, poverty and health: Exploring the connection. In I. Anderson, F. Baum, and M. Bentley (eds.), *Beyond bandaids: Exploring the underlying social determinants of Indigenous health* (pp. 77–90). Darwin, Australia: CRC for Aboriginal Health.

———. 2008. Lives of diversity: Indigenous Australians. *Australian Academy of the Social Sciences and the Bureau of Statistics Census Project*: Canberra.

———. 2009. An economy of poverty: Power and the domain of Aboriginality. *International Journal of Critical Indigenous Studies* 1(2):2–14.

———. 2010a. The nature of social science research. In M. Walter (ed.), *Social research methods: 2nd edition* (pp. 1–28). Melbourne: Oxford University Press.

———. 2010b. Participation action research. In M. Walter (ed.), *Social research methods.* Melbourne: Oxford University Press.

———. 2010c. The politics of the data: How the statistical Indigene is constructed. *International Journal of Critical Indigenous Studies* 3(2):45–56.

———. 2012. Keeping our distance: Non-indigenous/Aboriginal relations. In J. Pietsch and H. Aarons (eds.), *Australia: Identity, fear and governance in the 21st century.* Canberra, Australia: ANU E Press.

———, D. Habibis, and S. Taylor. 2011. How white is Australian social work? *Australian Social Work* 64(1):6–19.

Weaver, J. 2007. More light than heat: The current state of Native American studies. *American Indian Quarterly* 31(2):235.

West, E. 1998. Speaking towards an Aboriginal philosophy. Presentation to First Conference on Indigenous Philosophy, Linga Longa Philosophy Farm, NSW, April.

Western, J. 1969. What white Australians think. *Race* 10:411–434.

Wicihitowin: Circle of Shared Responsibility and Stewardship—Action Circles. wicihitowin.ca/action-circles (accessed March 4, 2012).

Wicihitowin: Circle of Shared Responsibility and Stewardship—History. wicihitowin.ca/history (accessed March 4, 2012).

Widdowson, F., and A. Howard. 2008. *Disrobing the Aboriginal industry: The deception behind indigenous cultural preservation.* Montreal: McGill-Queen's University Press.

Wilson, S. 2008. *Research as ceremony: Indigenous research methods.* Winnipeg, MB: Fernwood.

Wimmer, A. 2008. The making and unmaking of ethnic boundaries: A multilevel process theory. *American Journal of Sociology* 113(4):970–1022.

Wittgenstein, L. 1974. Philosophical investigations. Oxford: Blackwell.

Woodley, N. 2013. Gillard delivers 5th Closing the Gap report. The World Today with Eleanor Hall, February 6. www.abc.net.au/worldtoday/ content/2013/s3684374.htm (accessed March 19, 2013).

Your City, Your Voice. 2010. n.d. www.edmonton.ca/city_government/documents/PDF/ YCYV_report.pdf (accessed March 4, 2012).

Zuberi, T., and E. Bonilla-Silva. 2008. *White logic, white methods: Racism and methodology.* Lanham, MD: Rowman and Littlefield.

Index

Note: Figures and tables are indicated with an italicized page number followed by the letter *f* or *t*.

About the Authors

Maggie Walter (PhD) is a descendant of the trawlwoolway people from north-eastern Tasmania and is an Associate Professor at the School of Social Sciences, University of Tasmania. She publishes regularly across the field of social research methods and critical race relations. Maggie is currently Deputy Director of the National Indigenous Researcher and Knowledges Network (NIRAKN); an elected member of the Research Advisory Committee at the Australian Institute of Aboriginal and Torres Strait Islander Studies; a long-term steering committee member of the Longitudinal Study of Indigenous Children (LSIC), Australia's only national longitudinal Indigenous research program; and a member of the editorial board of the Native American and Indigenous Studies journal.

Chris Andersen (PhD) is Michif (Métis) and is an Associate Professor in the Faculty of Native Studies at the University of Alberta. He is the Director of the Rupertsland Centre for Métis Research. From a research perspective, he is interested in the ways in which the Canadian nation-state has created "identity" categories relating to Aboriginal communities and in particular the term Métis. Administratively, Chris has been on a number of national academic award adjudication committees, is a member of Statistics Canada's Advisory Committee on Social Conditions and of the Aboriginal and of the Northern Development Canada's Métis and Non-Status Indian Relations Directorate Research Advisory Circle, and is editor of the journal *aboriginal policy studies*.

green press

INITIATIVE

Left Coast Press, Inc. is committed to preserving ancient forests and natural resources. We elected to print this title on 30% post consumer recycled paper, processed chlorine free. As a result, for this printing, we have saved:

4 Trees (40' tall and 6-8" diameter)
1 Million BTUs of Total Energy
111 Pounds of Greenhouse Gases
606 Gallons of Wastewater
41 Pounds of Solid Waste

Left Coast Press, Inc. made this paper choice because our printer, Thomson-Shore, Inc., is a member of Green Press Initiative, a nonprofit program dedicated to supporting authors, publishers, and suppliers in their efforts to reduce their use of fiber obtained from endangered forests.

For more information, visit www.greenpressinitiative.org

Environmental impact estimates were made using the Environmental Defense Paper Calculator. For more information visit: www.papercalculator.org.